EUTHANASIA AND THE RIGHT TO DIE

A Comparative View

Jennifer M. Scherer
and
Rita J. Simon

ROWMAN & LITTLEFIELD PUBLISHERS, INC.
Lanham • Boulder • New York • Oxford

WMAN & LITTLEFIELD PUBLISHERS, INC.

Published in the United States of America
by Rowman & Littlefield Publishers, Inc.
4720 Boston Way, Lanham, Maryland 20706

12 Hid's Copse Road
Cumnor Hill, Oxford OX2 9JJ, England

British Library Cataloguing in Publication Information Available

Library of Congress Cataloging-in-Publication Data

Scherer, Jennifer M., 1964–
Euthanasia and the right to die : a comparative view / Jennifer M. Scherer and Rita J. Simon.
p. cm.
Includes bibliographical references and index.
ISBN 0-8476-9166-7 (cloth: alk. paper).—ISBN 0-8476-9167-5 (pbk: alk. paper)
1. Euthanasia—Cross-cultural studies. 2. Right to die—Cross-cultural studies. I. Simon, Rita James.
R726.S336 1999
179.7—dc21 98-41535
CIP

Printed in the United States of America

∞ ™ The paper used in this publication meets the minimum requirements of American National Standard for Information Sciences—Permanence of Paper for Printed Library Materials, ANSI Z39.48-1984.

Contents

Tables

Preface

Euthanasia and the Right to Die is the second in a series of volumes that examines a major public policy issue using an explicitly comparative approach. The organizing focus of the series is the analysis of important social issues about which many societies in the world have enacted laws and statutes and about which most of its members have opinions that they voice in the public arena. They are issues that receive extensive media coverage as well as judicial attention. The first volume focused on abortion. Subsequent topics may include marriage and divorce, drugs, citizenship, health care, and public education. Each volume should serve as a handbook containing empirical data and comprehensive references on the social issue or practice under study.

Euthanasia, at its most basic translation, means a "good death" or "dying well." The debates surrounding euthanasia and physician-assisted suicide have focused on the wish for control and influence over the manner and timing of one's death. The basic premise contrasts, on the one hand, the maintenance of personal dignity throughout the dying process and the relief of severe pain caused by terminal illness and, on the other hand, the potential for abuse by physicians, family members, health insurance companies, and society at large. These concerns are generally termed the "slippery slope," or wedge issues. In addition, the debate struggles with traditional religious doctrines, social mores, and philosophical attitudes concerning the value and meaning of life, the redemptive virtues of suffering, and the moral and societal taboos against the act of suicide, assisting suicide, or being directly involved in causing another individual's death.

To examine death and dying divorced from their many sociocultural milieus would be meaningless and inappropriate. Endeavoring to obtain a premature death through euthanasia or physician-assisted suicide is not solely the product of the progress that medical science has achieved; requests to hasten death also rely on the prevailing moral and political atmosphere of a society. As religion and religious institutions began to lose their guiding moral authority in society, laws piloting the conduct of individuals gradually grew more secular in nature, recognizing individual choice and personal freedoms.

In the chapters that follow, we explore these issues.

1

Death and Dying in a Historical Perspective

Dying has become an imposition upon humans, who seek to avoid it as they encounter the inevitably fatal aging process. But death has not always been thought of in this manner. Primitive societies, for instance, were more concerned with aspects of the here and now. The myths and symbols of these societies depict the realities of the actual world and the surrounding environment. Death, per se, was not considered a necessary characteristic of life.[1] The concept of death arose from culturally ingrained myths, rituals, and symbols when the individual was able to separate his or her identity from that of the tribe or the community as a whole. When death was thought of at all in these societies, it was most likely as the consequence of evil spirits imposed by either human foes or otherworldly demonic forces.[2]

As cultures developed more sophisticated perspectives, death became a central part of developing ideologies. Rationalizing and understanding the implications of one's death began to be discussed philosophically in Eastern and Western civilizations. In the Egyptian *Book of the Dead*, immortality of the soul was considered in depth, while in ancient Greece death became a topic of great interest among the noted philosophers of the time.[3] In the fifth and fourth centuries B.C., Greek philosophical debates about death focused primarily on what happened after death as opposed to the dying process or death itself. The point of contention was whether there was life after death or whether life was finalized by some type of annihilation.[4] Certain aspects of death, such as its significance and meaning as well as how to best care for the dying, were also considered within the realm of societal and political matters. Greek society was one of the first to be amenable to some forms of suicide, but qualifications applied and taboos existed against taking one's own life.[5] The term *euthanasia* was derived from the Greek *eu,* meaning well, and *thanatos,* meaning death. During this period, an emphasis began to be placed on a balance between physical fitness and mental well-being. Illness was viewed as a bothersome affliction, and an individual could seek the approval of the state to commit suicide. If approval was granted, the person was assisted by the magistrates, who supplied the poison.

Aristotle and Plato both advocated a crude sort of eugenics, recommending infanticide for deformed infants to ensure that only the best individuals inhabited the state.[6] Aristotle and Plato also supported euthanasia in cases of terminal or incurable illness. Each, however, rejected the notion of suicide. To Aristotle, suicide was an offense against the state, because man owed a civic duty to the state. Dishonor was attached to the surviving family, and a penalty was imposed (commonly the family was disfranchised). In addition, the right hand of the deceased was cut off and buried separately from the body.[7] Plato opposed suicide on the ground that "man is a soldier of God and must stay at his post until he calls."[8] Essentially, the Greeks brought the discussion of suicide into rational discourse and removed some of the superstitions previously attached to it.

Sophocles was probably the first to accept suicide as a general remedy for life's hardships and burdens. The Stoics readily embraced this position and tolerated suicide for a variety of reasons beyond incurable illness, including excruciating pain (not associated with an illness) and physical disabilities. Zeno, the founder of Stoicism, committed suicide because he severely twisted and injured a finger.[9] Death became a morally neutral issue, while suicide achieved a higher status. After the Roman conquest of Greece, the Stoic philosophy of death eventually dominated. In Rome, the idea of dying well was termed a *summum bonun,* and suicide was punishable only if it was irrational. It was also acceptable to end one's life because of a terminal illness, lunacy, or fear of dishonor.[10] For economic and military reasons, suicide was forbidden to soldiers, criminals, and slaves.

The Stoic attitude prevailed for two centuries after the death of Jesus. In the third century C.E., the growing influence of Christianity began to seriously erode the rational notions of suicide held up to this point. The Neoplatonists developed a new argument against suicide, one that hypothesized a disturbance of the soul and of the transition to the afterlife. But the fundamental Christian argument was that God had a sort of divine monopoly on human life. In other words, a human's life was the sole property of God, and it was his and only his to give and take. Suicide was an unforgivable transgression. Church and civil law were simultaneously affected by this new position. Church members who committed suicide would not be allowed Christian burials under any circumstance, even terminal illness, but were buried at a crossroads on a highway. Their property and goods were confiscated and became the property of the state.

In the fifth century, St. Augustine became an influential theological commentator on suicide. He declared that suicide violated the function of church and state and that it was against the Sixth Commandment, "Thou shalt not kill." According to St. Augustine, human suffering was decreed by God, and it was the responsibility of man to bear his burden.[11] The impact of St. Augustine's views would be felt for almost a thousand years and go largely uncontested. In the thirteenth century, St. Thomas Aquinas further developed the theological arguments against suicide in his *Summa Theologica*. According to Aquinas, suicide was the worst sin an individual could commit because it left no time for repentance and was contrary to natural law. Drawing on Aristotle (who rejected suicide on the basis of man's civic duty), Aquinas believed that suicide was unlawful because man belongs to his community. Drawing on Plato (who rejected suicide because man is a soldier of God), Aquinas held that suicide went against God because life was a gift from God and subject only to God's discretion. Drawing on the Neoplatonists (who believed that suicide disturbs the soul and its passage to the afterlife), Aquinas held that suicide perturbs the soul.[12]

The Renaissance did not alter orthodox attitudes toward suicide, but it allowed for the emergence of enlightened views, and educated opinion once again began to perceive the Greek and Roman concept of an "easy death" as something for which to strive. What allowed this transition was the renewed emphasis and interest in individualism. Ironically, in *Utopia*, which the noted Catholic Sir Thomas More penned in 1516, patients residing in an ideal society were encouraged to commit suicide if they were suffering from an incurable disease or were experiencing great pain.[13] The wishes of those patients who did not choose euthanasia were respected as well. In 1626, Frances Bacon wrote *New Atlantis*, in which he described a physician's duty as easing pain not only when the patient is expected to recover but also during the stages of dying.[14] John Donne, in 1647, argued that suicide was not inherently evil and that it was not incongruous with the laws of nature, reason, and God.[15] Voltaire, Rousseau, and Montaigne believed suicide was a just and reasonable cause. The Renaissance served to make the lay public more informed and aware of general humanitarian issues; for the first time physicians also began to recognize their responsibility to the patient and emphasized more humane manners of treating the terminally ill patient.[16]

In 1757, David Hume's essay "On Suicide" refuted St. Thomas Aquinas's essay "Whether It Is Lawful to Kill Oneself" from *Summa*

Theologica. Hume discredited Aquinas's notion of God's established order because human lives are governed by general causal laws, as is all matter in the universe. In essence, what Hume asked was, since persons die from natural causes, why is unnatural divine intervention necessary? He also refuted the idea that man must play a passive role in the context of natural occurrences and believed that man could not survive by doing so. He held that suicide was not necessarily a sin and, further, that it was not a crime. He believed that man has a "native liberty" to determine the circumstances of his death, including that of pain and disease. Hume also noted that nowhere in the Scriptures is suicide expressly prohibited.[17]

In the latter half of the nineteenth century, suicide began to be examined scientifically. There was growing curiosity about the biological causes of suicide. Speculation ranged from a genetic defect to a chemical imbalance in the brain. In 1897, Emile Durkheim examined suicide as a social fact and correlated it with particular sociocultural aspects, such as being Protestant or residing in a certain geographical locale.[18] He attributed the majority of suicides to social maladaption and divided suicide into three types: egoistic, altruistic, and anomic. Egoistic suicide is characterized by the individual not being able to identify with society. In altruistic suicide, the individual overidentifies with society. Anomic suicide occurs when the individual experiences despair and demoralization. Durkheim's work was influential in altering the way suicide was studied and forced researchers to consider the possibility that the act was subject to societal forces beyond the control of the individual.

Sigmund Freud believed that suicide was the result of an inversion of the *thanatos* (death) instinct in emotionally immature individuals. Interestingly, Freud was himself a recipient of euthanasia.[19] He was suffering extreme pain from cancer of the jaw and asked his physician to provide a lethal injection, which his physician did.

By the beginning of the twentieth century, discussion of euthanasia and suicide began to focus on action rather than academic debate. In 1906, a bill introduced into the Ohio legislature supported the act of euthanasia. The bill was met with intense criticism from the press and provoked much debate. The *New York Times* on February 3, 1906, ran an editorial likening the practice of euthanasia in the United States to that of more barbaric types of societies. The Ohio bill was ultimately defeated in committee, but it received nearly 25 percent of the committee vote. That the bill was proposed at all indicates that the general populace was concerned with the circumstances of the terminally ill patient and the dying process.

In 1935, legislation was introduced in England supporting the legalization of euthanasia. The British Voluntary Euthanasia Society came into existence solely to promote this legislation. The bill had its origin in a speech given in 1931 by Dr. C. Killick Millard before the Society of Officers of Health. In his talk, Dr. Millard addressed the legalization of euthanasia and proposed the voluntary euthanasia legalization bill, which set forth guidelines to allow any terminally ill individual experiencing significant pain to obtain a euthanasia permit, with which the person could procure a lethal dose of a drug. The lethal dose of medication could be administered by a physician or by the patient. In 1936, the bill was defeated in the House of Lords. The British Voluntary Euthanasia Society continued to fight for the rights of terminally ill patients, to propose euthanasia legislation, and to raise awareness of the issue.[20]

The Euthanasia Society of America was formed in 1938 in part because of the failure of the euthanasia legislation in England. At about the same time, mercy killings were beginning to be recognized by the public as a way of taking control of desperate situations that the legal and medical systems had failed to address. A grand jury in New York refused to indict Harry Johnson on charges of first-degree murder after he killed his cancer-stricken wife, who had begged him to take her life. The grand jury heard testimony from three psychiatrists, who determined that Johnson was temporarily insane at the time of the crime.[21] After reading of a mercy-killing case with similarities to his own situation, Louis Repouille killed his "incurable imbecile" son with chloroform because he could not stand to see his son suffer any longer. The boy was deformed, mute, blind, and suffering from a brain tumor. The jury convicted Repouille of manslaughter in the second degree, but the judge suspended the sentence.[22]

Public opinion data from the United States and the United Kingdom reflect the attitudes and beliefs of the late 1930s. When the American public was asked, Do you favor mercy deaths under government supervision for hopelessly ill individuals? nearly 39 percent of those polled in 1936 agreed with the statement and, in 1939, 41 percent did.[23] In two Gallup polls administered in 1937 and 1939, the percentages that supported euthanasia were slightly higher (46 percent).[24] In the United Kingdom, a similar poll revealed that almost 70 percent supported euthanasia.[25]

One of the greatest setbacks to the pro-euthanasia movement was Adolf Hitler's unfortunate choice of the word *euthanasia* for his mass extermination program prior to and during World War II. Approximately 100,000 men, women, and children who were physically handicapped, mentally disabled, or genetically inferior became victims of Hitler's eugenics or racial purification program. The extent to which human rights were violated and the ruthless manner in which the program was conducted stunned the world. One of Hitler's first steps in his racial purification program was the enactment of a law in 1933 that made sterilization of individuals compulsory if any heredity illnesses were present. Individuals chosen for this program had no choice but to submit to the operation. Hitler furthered his nationalistic indoctrination program through the education of all German health workers with racial cleansing or eugenics theories. By the onset of World War II, the messages had begun to take effect, and the Germans were ready to accept the idea that those who could not aid the war effort were essentially useless and better off dead.

The killing began in 1939. Typically, the patients were ushered into shower stalls on the pretense that they were to wash, but instead lethal gas was administered through the shower nozzles. The state informed the deceased's living relatives of the death with a letter stating that the patient had died "unexpectedly" and then produced a fake death certificate.[26] Suspicion grew as many families received death certificates that contained obvious lies. Death certificates might state that the patient died during an operation to correct a deformity that the family knew did not exist. Further, individuals residing close to the death facilities started to complain about the stench from the smokestacks. In an effort to quell these claims, Nazi officials claimed that mass cremations were necessary because of deadly epidemics.

Rampant rumors began affecting the morale of the German citizenry and the soldiers at the front. The elderly feared that they would be the next "useless" group in line for extermination. Soldiers heard stories that soldiers who suffered head wounds were euthanized upon returning home from the front. In 1941, Hitler instituted the law of existence, which publicly announced his belief in the destruction of lesser individuals so that the remaining, superior, individuals might live better.[27] Bowing to pressure from the clergy, physicians, and other groups concerned with the morality of the law and the severe infractions against fundamental human rights, Hitler slowed the program, although the killing did not come to a complete halt (as many believed). The elimination of defective children continued for four more years.[28]

It is important to note that Hitler's euthanasia program never had the goal of providing physician-assisted suicide to a terminally ill patient or a patient with an incurable disease. All of the killings were committed without the patient's consent and without the patient being aware of the impending act. Hitler's definition of euthanasia is far from historical and present day interpretations of the term.

Directly following World War II, discussion of euthanasia practices largely came to a standstill as the world attempted to rebuild itself and recover from the war. Gradually, the tragedies and atrocities that had occurred in Germany and German-occupied Europe during the preceding years came to light. The nations of the world wondered how this could have happened in such an advanced society. In 1947, a Gallup poll revealed Americans' opposition to euthanasia: only 37 percent of the respondents agreed with the statement, When a person has a disease that cannot be cured, do you think doctors should be allowed by law to end the patient's life by some painless means if the patient and his family request it? This is a significant decline from the 1937 and 1939 Gallup polls, which showed a 46 percent approval rate.

Increased legislation, scholarly works, and debate characterized the euthanasia movement of the 1950s. In England, Lord Chorley introduced a motion into the House of Lords that basically restated the position that the Euthanasia Society had previously proposed. The motion was withdrawn due to a lack of support and was eventually reintroduced in 1962 and 1969. In the United States, the Euthanasia Society in New York, which had strong support from the clergy, physicians, and the general public, tried to gain legislative support for its bill. Its efforts failed largely due to the refusal of the Senate president to act. Undaunted, the society decided to redirect its efforts toward public education.

Important scholarly works also surfaced in the early 1950s. One of the most influential and controversial was an article in *Theology Today* by Joseph Fletcher, a prominent Protestant ethicist.[29] Fletcher supported the bill the Euthanasia Society presented to the New York legislature, and his article responded to criticisms generally leveled at the practice of euthanasia. Fletcher disagreed with the definition of euthanasia as murder. Whereas the crime of murder required "malice aforethought," euthanasia was a case of "mercy aforethought." He further argued that, although euthanasia may be premeditated and deliberate (as is murder), it should be considered an excusable or justifiable act without the presence of malice.[30] Fletcher believed that the biblical commandment "Thou shalt not kill" had been wrongly interpreted. It should be understood as one should not unlawfully kill another individual. He also held that suicide is justifiable when particular characteristics are present in the person considering euthanasia. These include knowledge, self-possession, and control.

Before the 1960s, many physicians did not disclose a terminal illness to the patient. But studies showed that patients wanted to be informed of their medical diagnosis and treatment options. A 1962 Canadian survey revealed that nine out of ten individuals would rather die suddenly than from a protracted illness, even if it meant dying earlier. Nearly 73 percent of those questioned favored euthanasia.[31]

A 1964–65 national opinion poll in England of 2,000 general practitioners selected from the *Medical Register* found that nearly 50 percent of these physicians said that a dying patient had requested final relief from suffering; 54 percent believed that this request was discordant with existing laws; 76 percent stated that some physicians did provide treatment that precipitated the onset of death; and 36 percent said they would perform voluntary euthanasia if it were legally sanctioned.[32] In 1969, the British Medical Association, following the lead of the World Medical Association, passed a resolution stating its opposition to euthanasia. In 1967, in the United States, attorney Luis Kutner, in conjunction with members of the Euthanasia Society, developed the original living will. During this period, the Euthanasia Education Council was also created.

In 1970, public opinion data showed that more than 50 percent of those polled believed that life should not be unnecessarily extended; and a survey of Seattle physicians showed that almost 60 percent would practice euthanasia if it were formally legalized.[33] In 1973, 53 percent of those polled answered yes to the question, When a person has a disease that cannot be cured, do you think doctors should be allowed by law to end the patient's life by some painless means if the patient and his family request it?[34] In a 1975 poll, 87 percent of the respondents favored passive euthanasia, and 63 percent believed that patients with incurable illness had the right to request and receive medication that would end their lives.[35]

In 1971 and 1973, the states of Washington and Wisconsin introduced death-with-dignity bills, which were unsuccessful because they did not gain sufficient sponsorship. In 1973, 1974, and 1975, Massachusetts, Delaware, Maryland, and Virginia presented bills to their legislatures attempting to legalize the living will. The bills were shelved due to either strong opposition or lack of support. Also in 1973, the American Hospital Association created the Patient's Bill of Rights, which includes the right to refuse treatment and the right of informed consent. In September 1976, California passed the Natural Death Act, which legitimizes the living will. It was the first U.S. right-to-die statute. In 1977, treatment refusal laws were passed in Arkansas, Idaho, Nevada, New Mexico, North Carolina, Oregon, and Texas.

In other countries, euthanasia societies were forming to advance the discussion of death with dignity and patient rights. In 1973, the first voluntary euthanasia societies in the Netherlands were established. Three years later, Japan and Germany both formed voluntary euthanasia societies, and the first international conference of the societies was held in Tokyo in 1976. The following year, the Dutch Medical Council officially accepted voluntary euthanasia.

In 1975, awareness of the emotional needs and economic considerations of the patient's family peaked in the United States with the case of Karen Ann Quinlan, a case that demonstrates the conflict among the law, the medical community, and the wishes of the comatose or permanently unconscious patient's family. On April 15, 1975, Quinlan collapsed from respiratory arrest induced by mixing drugs and alcohol and lapsed into a permanent vegetative state, unable to breathe without the aid of a respirator or eat without a feeding tube. Her appointed physician maintained that, although she had irreparable brain damage, she was not technically brain-dead by the Harvard Medical School criteria, noting her response to stimuli, involuntary muscle activity, and a non-flat electroencephalogram. Quinlan's father believed that she would not want to be kept alive through such extraordinary measures with no hope of recovery and signed a release to turn off the respirator keeping her alive. But the physicians refused to turn off the respirator, believing that to do so would be an act of homicide.

Quinlan's parents subsequently undertook a prolonged legal battle to remove her from the life-support system. The Superior Court decided that she did not meet the Harvard criteria for brain death and found in favor of the hospital. The Quinlans appealed this decision to the New Jersey Supreme Court, which overturned the lower court's ruling and allowed for the removal of the life support. But artificial feeding was maintained, and Quinlan remained "alive" until 1985, when she died from the complications of pneumonia. A major issue in the ruling was the patient's right to privacy and the ability of the guardian to assert the right on behalf of the patient. The Quinlan case garnered wide coverage from the media, elevating public awareness of the issue, and the phrase right to die began to be used with many death and dying issues. The only right that the court confirmed in the Quinlan case was the "right under certain circumstances to be disconnected from artificial life support systems, or . . . the right-to-die a natural death."[36] Public opinion and legislation revolving around caring for patients were profoundly effected by the Quinlan case. Fifty bills were introduced in almost forty states in 1977. Currently, in thirty-six states, assisted suicide is criminalized by statute, and in eight states it is criminalized by common law.

In 1980, the pro-euthanasia group Scottish Exit (now known as the Voluntary Euthanasia Society of Scotland) released the first guide to suicide in the world. Also in 1980, Derek Humphry, a leading euthanasia advocate, founded the Hemlock Society. Humphry has a strong emotional tie to the debate: in the late 1970s, he assisted his first wife, who was suffering from cancer, with suicide. In 1981, he published *Let Me Die before I Wake*, which examined the issues surrounding suicide and the terminally ill patient. He later founded the Euthanasia Research and Guidance Organization Group. The World Federation of Right-to-

Die Societies was formed in 1980, with eighteen countries participating. In the Netherlands, a Rotterdam court stated the conditions under which assisted suicide and voluntary euthanasia would not lead to prosecution. In 1984, the Supreme Court of the Netherlands declared that voluntary euthanasia was acceptable provided that certain guidelines were strictly followed.

Even though the general public had become enlightened with respect to patient rights and issues of dying, a great deal of confusion still existed at hospitals as to the specific guidelines. Many hospitals attempted to implement official, standardized policies. In an effort to standardize their policy, the Los Angeles County Medical Association and the Los Angeles County Bar Association jointly developed a set of guidelines detailing the circumstances under which a physician could withdraw life-support systems without prior court approval. A life-support mechanism could be stopped if the patient had previously signed a directive requesting that his or her life not be artificially maintained. Life support could also be withheld if two physicians determined that the patient had suffered irreversible cessation of brain function and was brain-dead prior to the system being disconnected. Life support could also stop with a diagnosis of irreversible coma if the patient had previously requested not to be maintained on indefinite life support. The patient's guardian must also agree with the decision to cease life-support systems.[37] Many other hospitals and associations implemented their own sets of guidelines. The *Hastings Center Report* found, however, that only a small number of physicians followed the guidelines; 5 percent of physicians said they would withhold fluids and food from the patient, and about 20 percent would stop providing antibiotics.[38]

A 1995 survey of Oregon physicians found that 60 percent felt that assisted suicide should be legal in some cases, and 66 percent said it would be ethical in some cases; 33 percent believed that assisted suicide was immoral, 34 percent said it violated professional ethics, and 30 percent said it violated personal beliefs.[39] In 1994–95, a similar survey was administered to Michigan physicians, who were asked if they would be likely to participate in a suicide if a patient requested it, if it were legal, and if all the legal guidelines were met. Twenty-two percent responded that they "might be willing to participate with either the patient or physician taking the final action." In addition, 13 percent said they would be willing to participate in a suicide but only if "the patient takes the final action."[40]

In 1990, the U.S. Supreme Court ruled in the Nancy Cruzan case that, for patients in a comatose or vegetative state, life support and medical treatment may be suspended if there is clear and convincing evidence that this is the action the patient would have requested if she could have done so.[41] It further recognized that the right to refuse medical treatment is protected by the Constitution. In response to the Cruzan case, the Patient Self-Determination Act was passed by Congress. The act requires that such facilities as nursing homes and hospitals provide patients with information on their state laws regarding advance directives. This act also compels hospitals to respect the patient's living will.

A pivotal figure in the right-to-die movement in the United States is Dr. Jack Kevorkian, who has assisted in almost a hundred suicides. His medical license was suspended shortly after he began his highly publicized campaign for legalized assisted suicide. Kevorkian was twice prosecuted for murder before dismissal of the charges in both cases led the state of Michigan to pass a specially designed law to prevent physician-assisted dying. This eventually resulted in Kevorkian's imprisonment. He responded with a hunger strike and refused to cooperate in any manner, fostering a great amount of attention from the media. The opposition arranged for Kevorkian's release to prevent him from becoming a martyr for the cause.[42] Later, Kevorkian faced charges for assisting a rural Michigan woman, ill with multiple sclerosis, with suicide. Janet Good, founder of the Michigan Hemlock Society, was indicted by the same grand jury, as she was present at the suicide. The judge released Kevorkian on a personal bond after Kevorkian promised not to participate in any other suicides until the charges were resolved. A mistrial was subsequently declared due to statements made that had tainted the jury.

The Oregon Death with Dignity Act of 1994 was passed by a margin of 52 percent to 48 percent. The law allowed physicians to prescribe lethal drugs for the purpose of assisted suicide. The law was unable to take effect immediately due to an injunction and came under appeal to the U.S. Supreme Court. In October 1997, the Court decided not to hear the appeal and ordered the dismissal of the lawsuit, thus upholding the original law.[43] On April 23, 1997, the Oregon House Committee on Judiciary, Subcommittee on Family Law, voted to repeal the Oregon Death with Dignity Act. The House Judiciary subcommittee decided to place a measure on the ballot in November 1997 asking the voters if they wanted the physician-assisted suicide law repealed.[44]

Oregon Governor John Kitzhaber, himself a physician, came out in favor of physician-assisted suicide during the election year. He had opposed the bill in 1994 but had altered his position, stating that individuals should be able to freely make end-of-life decisions. The voter referendum was accomplished via a vote-by-mail referendum and drew a heavy response. By a margin of 60 to 40 percent, voters in Oregon paved the way for the first assisted-suicide law in the nation.[45] The election's outcome was considered critical for the U.S. right-to-die movement. At this writing, four terminally ill individuals have died under the new law. The law has thus far been used sparingly because of the threat of federal prosecution under drug control laws. In June 1998, Attorney General Janet Reno announced that the U.S. Justice Department would not punish those involved in prescribing drugs for the euthanasia procedure.[46]

The U.S. Supreme Court determined in mid-1997 that the Constitution does not provide for a right to assistance from a physician in hastening death for a terminally ill patient.[47] The Court heard appeals from the states of Washington and New York, where it had previously determined that a terminally ill patient who is mentally competent has a constitutional right to physician-assisted suicide. The states wanted to sustain their existing laws, which have been on the books since the nineteenth century, that make it illegal for anyone (including a physician) to assist someone to commit suicide. In *Compassion in Dying v. Washington*, the Ninth U.S. Circuit Court held that the patient has a privacy right to assisted suicide under the Constitution's guarantee of due process. In *Quill v. Vacco*, the Second Circuit Court of New York held that terminally ill patients have the right to hasten death through the use of drugs, just as other patients have the right to refuse artificial life supports under the Constitution's equal protection guarantee.[48]

2

The Fundamental Issues

Semantics plays a confusing role in the right-to-die movement. Often, terms associated with the issue are used incorrectly or are misinterpreted or misunderstood. The word *euthanasia* in its most basic translation simply means a "good death" or "dying well." The term has been frequently used to refer to the hastening or quickening of a severely ill person's death, otherwise know as mercy killing. The field, however, recognizes an array of sophisticated categories of euthanasia. Passive euthanasia refers to the natural death of a patient through the disconnection of life-support equipment or cessation of life-sustaining medical procedures, such as feeding. Active euthanasia involves a deliberate action to end the life of a suffering patient. Active voluntary euthanasia (sometimes known as voluntary active euthanasia) pertains to an intervention, such as lethal injection, requested by a mentally competent, suffering patient so as to precipitate death.

Active involuntary euthanasia involves the intervention by a physician to cause the death of the patient *without* the individual's informed consent. This is one of the most controversial and least socially accepted forms of euthanasia. In a physician-assisted suicide, a doctor provides the means for the patient to commit suicide. In assisted suicide, an individual other than the physician provides the patient the means to commit suicide. These means may be a certain quantity of drugs that the individual intends to use to end his or her life. The term *self-deliverance* is preferred by some over the term *suicide,* so as not to correlate the two events, because they believe they are entirely different, with self-deliverance stemming from a rational choice and traditional suicide resulting from emotional or psychological trauma. Palliative care is the management of pain and discomfort, without medical treatment that is curative in nature.

Considerations Regarding Suicide

The primary arguments against the act of suicide assert that humans are by nature social creatures with responsibilities to society, to each other, to the self, and to certain standards of behavior generally regarded as dignified. Thus a major contention is that suicide is a crime against society. In this view, individuals are indebted to society for their existence and must perform certain social duties in return for the benefits that society provides. By committing suicide, individuals renege on this commitment.

The Enlightenment philosopher Jean-Jacques Rousseau explored the relationship between the individual and society. According to him, there are two types of freedom: natural freedom and social freedom. Natural freedom is freedom in the state of nature, in which one can do as one pleases. Individuals give up natural freedom when they become bound together in a society for the greater benefits that social freedom provides. Social freedom is the freedom to realize the will of the collective, which takes precedence over the individual wills within the collective. Individuals have the free will to do what the general will wants them to do. If individuals do not abide by the general will, they will suffer repercussions because the social structure cannot sustain too many actions that go against the collective. The social structure requires certain behaviors of its members in order to endure. Emile Durkeim furthered this notion by saying that society is a complex organism that springs from our collective life, gaining an existence and momentum of its own. Once established, society turns and confronts its creators, demanding a measure of obedience. A stable society needs productive, creative, and capable individuals who are not completely self-oriented to maintain the collective as a cohesive entity.

This argument is sometimes countered by querying the exact nature of the duties that individuals supposedly owe society and determining if these duties are merely dependent upon social status. The above argument suggests that all members of society have an equal stake in the functioning of society and the distribution of resources, which is by no means true.

A second argument that is often advanced against suicide is that it inflicts pain, suffering, and hardship on the deceased's relatives and friends. When considering this argument, it must be realized that in almost every instance suicide is committed only after tremendous consideration about others and the possible harm they may suffer. However, in a Durkheimian sense, it is often the case that an individual who commits suicide is already isolated from family, friends, and others.

Suicide is also held to be a crime against God. Some believe that it is in violation of an obligation or responsibility we owe to God as his creations; others construe it to be a breach of the Sixth Commandment, "Thou shalt not kill." This proposal, of course, is dependent upon individual beliefs and upon interpretations of Scripture. Some individuals also consider suicide cowardly, since death relieves the individual from responsibilities and duties. A morally sound person, the argument goes, would face these challenges with courage. Yet another argument against suicide is that it is unnatural. Because the term has several vague meanings and interpretations, it is difficult to decipher its precise definition. To deem something unnatural does not necessarily imply that it is inherently bad or evil; it simply implies that it is contrary to the usual or accepted course of nature. Finally, some believe that suicide is an insult to basic human dignity. The obvious rebuttal is that there are far more heinous deeds than suicide. Is life really above death, when one is suffering the tortures of advanced throat cancer, when one is slowly suffocating, or when one is subjected to extreme physical and mental brutality and persecution as a political prisoner? A wide range of factors must be considered when determining the rightness or wrongness of suicide.

Those who support the right to die generally believe that euthanasia and assisted suicide should be legalized and recognized as morally acceptable and that guidelines and safeguards can prevent the downward descent on the "slippery slope" of abuse. Those who oppose euthanasia and assisted suicide hold that these acts should never be options for anyone, regardless of circumstances. Finally, there are those in the middle, who believe that there are certain extreme circumstances under which euthanasia or assisted suicide could be justified but, nevertheless, hold that the law should not be altered. They believe that the court system is capable of handling such rare and isolated situations and that no formal legislation is required.

The Proponents' Position

Proponents of euthanasia and assisted suicide ground their position in two basic principles: self-determination and mercy, or compassion. These concepts are used in conjunction to develop broad-based arguments or, conversely, are presented in isolation to emphasize the significance of that particular concept, since each of these guiding principles appeals to a fundamental sense of individual rights and constitutional guarantees.

The Concept of Self-Determination

Implicit in the concept of self-determination is the right of individuals to control and dictate the course of their own lives. It assumes autonomy and the freedom to be self-governing with respect to choices concerning the self and one's own well-being. Consequently, decisions that individuals make affecting the course of their lives should be respected as long as they do not threaten, injure, or harm others. The right to self-determination applies, according to proponents, to one's medical decisions, as well, including the circumstances and nature of one's death. Allowing the individual to control this process permits a patient with a terminal illness to die in a dignified manner, can prevent extended suffering from intractable pain, and serves to psychologically relieve the mind of the individual, who knows that the option of a painless death is available.[1] When the alternatives are either a peaceful death with dignity and compassion or a death accompanied by unbearable, untreatable pain and distress, proponents believe common sense and human kindness prescribe that the choice belongs to the individual.

Everyone has a natural, biological obligation or right to die, but what proponents support is the right to control the conditions under which one's death transpires. Some proponents simply want to ensure that there will not be state or church interference in decisions about such a fundamental, highly personal issue as dying.[2] Individual control over the dying process serves to accommodate diverse viewpoints on the meanings and values concerning life and death. Values and belief systems on the meaning and significance of life and death differ dramatically among individuals, so institutions should not impose a universal value system upon everyone.[3] By legalizing euthanasia and assisted suicide, an option would then exist for those who choose to exercise their right in accordance with their personal values and beliefs. The needs of those who do not hold these same values and beliefs would also be met by continuing to provide medical treatment and pain control until death occurs naturally.

The patient's right to autonomy in the area of passive euthanasia has been established in U.S. legal decisions since the beginning of the twentieth century. In 1914, *Schloendorff v. New York Hospital* found that the plaintiff had the right to refuse medical treatment. Justice Benjamin Cardozo stated that "every human being of adult years and sound mind has a right to determine what shall be done with his own body."[4] The principle was even more strongly asserted in the 1970s cases of Yetter and Perlmutter.[5] In these cases it was held that competent adults, excluding those with communicable diseases who pose health risks to the public at large and some situations in which individuals have dependents, have the right to refuse medical treatment, on personal grounds or for religious reasons, even if it means that they will die.

Later cases involving Jehovah's Witnesses further established the right to refuse some parts of treatment but to allow others. Other documents such as advanced directives and living wills stating the desire to refuse treatment in certain medical instances became legally recognized and permitted passive euthanasia when a competent individual had made the request before the onset of the illness. These applied even if the patient had technically become incompetent afterward. Furthermore, a durable power of attorney allows an individual to appoint a relative or close friend to make decisions about receiving or refusing treatment should the individual no longer be competent to make such choices. This legal recourse serves to protect the self-determination rights of the individual but only with respect to passive euthanasia, not active euthanasia or physician-assisted suicide.

Mercy, Compassion, and the Treatment of Pain

The second element of the proponents' argument is the concept of mercy and compassion. For many individuals, the quality of life is important, not the sanctity of life or its length. If the quality of life is reduced to an unacceptable level, if an acceptable level will never be regained because of an incurable, debilitating illness, extreme suffering, or loss of personal dignity, then proponents argue that individuals should have the right to seek assistance from a physician in ending their lives. Individuals are essentially asserting the right to make a judgment on the value or worth of life to them based on their values and belief systems. The principle of mercy in the euthanasia debate rests on the notions of compassion, understanding, and kindness toward patients who suffer from intractable, untreatable, or intolerable pain. In terms of euthanasia, mercy is granted by providing direct assistance in dying or letting patients die through voluntary active euthanasia, voluntary passive euthanasia, or physician-assisted suicide.

The issue of pain and suffering among terminally ill patients is subject to great medical and moral debate as well. While it is the aim of the medical profession to assist patients through extreme and unrelievable pain, the controversy lies in how to most effectively treat the pain without subjecting patients to greater harm. The physician's *Hippocratic Corpus* states foremost that a physician should "first, do no harm." From the proponents' perspective, this clause can be interpreted to mean that no additional pain and suffering will be caused and that the physician must seek to end any present pain and suffering.[6]

To not inflict any additional pain and suffering, the physician may have to forgo certain treatments and procedures that would not specifically provide a greater benefit to the patient. In addition, if treatment is unlikely to greatly extend the life of the patient without causing undue pain in the process, it would also be considered merciful if treatment was withheld and the patient allowed to die. Relieving pain is possible in the majority of instances, but complete pain control still eludes medical treatment. There are also cases in which pain management is possible but does not occur because of patients' circumstances. For example, patients may be physically unable to communicate the extent of their pain or may be afraid or hesitant to request additional painkillers. Other individuals may reside in remote areas where no pain management resources or skilled care providers exist. Or pain relief may not be provided due to lack of training, inexperience, insufficient resources, or concerns about addiction on the part of the attending health care providers. In the worst-case scenario, pain can be controlled by sedating patients into an unconscious state. However, proponents of euthanasia and assisted suicide contend this is almost equivalent to death insofar as patients are not conscious or functioning on an independent level.

The oaths that physicians and other medical practitioners take may be interpreted as ethically and morally binding, committing them to certain duties and responsibilities. In some instances, simply adhering to one's duty will resolve an ethical problem. In other instances, performing one's duty will occasion an ethical dilemma because two duties may seem in conflict, and one duty will have to be subjugated to the other. One of the sworn duties that is rarely superseded by another is that of nonmaleficence: First, do no harm.

While the application of this directive may seem straightforward, its exercise is complicated in the case of euthanasia and assisted suicide, especially when the physician regards hastening death, either actively or passively, as harmful. But other physicians believe that allowing patients to suffer unduly and to linger for weeks in excruciating pain waiting to die is also causing harm. The physician may perhaps best resolve this ethical dilemma by following the patient's desires stated in any existing advance directives or by consulting with the patient and family simultaneously as to the best course of action. The questions of self-determination and autonomy in these instances are controversial: complying with the desires of the patient actually may cause harm, for although the competent patient maintains the right to make autonomous decisions about treatment received or refused, this does not necessarily translate into the right to irreversibly forgo this autonomy by receiving a lethal injection. The ultimate outcome of euthanasia is death, and thus freedom of choice is forever relinquished.

Under the principles of deontology, physicians theoretically also have the duty of beneficence. This duty encompasses not only doing no harm to the patient but doing good as well. Like that of nonmaleficence, the duty of beneficence is sometimes subjectively applied in the case of euthanasia and relief of pain and suffering. Some physicians believe that relieving the patient of extreme pain is a virtuous act, even if it means administering a lethal injection. On the other hand, causing the premature death of a patient for any reason is considered wrong and, thus, nonbeneficient.

The euthanasia discourse also turns on the availability and the implementation of palliative care, the true number of patients affected by untreatable pain, and the best method of pain management. Pain treatment for terminally ill patients has serious shortcomings. Even with advanced medical technologies and wonder drugs, pain cannot always be managed effectively.[7] Near the end of a terminal illness, the patient may experience a wide range of distressing symptoms, including disfigurement, incontinence, paralysis, weakness, loss of control of bodily functions, suffocation, blindness, acute nausea, and extreme psychological anguish. Many of these patients experience extreme pain and suffering as a result of inadequate treatment for pain relief, despite the fact that effective remedies exist. In part, this is due to the fact that some providers are not trained properly in the administration of drugs for pain relief or are simply unaware of state-of-the-art treatments.[8] With respect to the success of palliative care, even considering recent significant medical advances, up to 5 percent of patients do not experience reduction in pain to a tolerable level.[9]

Another controversial area of pain treatment has to do with the amount of pain-relief medication necessary to alleviate the pain. Some physicians are concerned with the patient becoming addicted to the painkiller if too much is administered and if ever-higher doses are required to ease the pain. Proponents ridicule this argument in light of the fact that the patient is already terminally ill and is almost assuredly going to die within six months regardless of an addiction problem. The possibility of an addiction problem developing should be overlooked when examining the long-term prognosis of the patient.

Advancements in science, medical technology, and pharmaceuticals have resulted in a prolonged life expectancy. Unfortunately, surviving longer through the final stages of an illness may not always be desirable when life has deteriorated to the point of being kept alive via artificial means or existing in a physical state that most would consider unacceptable. Proponents believe that patients should not be subjected to extensive, prolonged suffering if they deem that the burdens of their illness greatly outweigh their quality of life. An extended life does not always translate into a desirable or acceptable existence. Euthanasia and assisted suicide are alternatives that permit patients to end their suffering when the time is right and to die in a peaceful, dignified, and relatively pain-free manner.

The Opponents' Position

Slippery Slope, or Wedge, Concerns

Opponents of euthanasia and assisted suicide believe that one of the greatest areas for potential abuse and misuse of euthanasia practices lies within medical and institutional establishments. They further hold that euthanasia and assisted-suicide decisions go beyond individual rights, since the participation of another party (by either the actual commission of the act or by providing patients the means for completion of the act) turns the death into a social consideration and must, therefore, adhere to the norms, standards, and laws of the community.[10] The physician may also suffer guilt from causing the death of another, failure due to an inability to find a cure, remorse for the patient, social stigmatization, and even legal ramifications.

Those against euthanasia and assisted suicide also believe that one person (a physician) or one profession (medicine) should not be accorded a Godlike power over the life and death decisions of other individuals.[11] Physicians who swear to abide by the Hippocratic oath are charged with healing patients, not harming or killing them.[12] Patients may lose trust in their physicians and question the physicians' primary motives for a treatment regimen, knowing that the physician has a dual capability—to cure and to cause death. In addition, the manipulation of this power in certain circumstances could lead to dangerous situations in which there is a diminished respect for human life and acceptance or approval of nonvoluntary forms of euthanasia.

Concerns also arise because of the possibility of a misdiagnosis or a faulty prognosis for recovery. Physicians can (and do) make erroneous medical decisions or arrive at premature conclusions, which could cause patients to misjudge their conditions and to elect euthanasia or assisted suicide when in fact their illness could be curable. Physicians may also frighten patients into thinking that they will experience considerably more pain than they actually will and that a natural death will be excruciating, when in reality the majority of natural deaths are not thought to be painful.[13] Although instances of misdiagnosis and defective prognosis may be rare, opponents say even one error is too many.

Another fear stems from the possibility of physicians using euthanasia to cover up medical mistakes that would subject them to malpractice lawsuits or to disguise the fact that they did not provide adequate treatment. Opponents believe that, for unscrupulous physicians, euthanasia would be a relatively easy answer to such situations. Unfortunately, the fact that physicians have the weight of professional authority and knowledge behind their decisions makes patients more susceptible to following their orders. This part of the physician-patient relationship can be a very influential factor in the decision-making process, especially when the patient is terminally ill and in a compromised situation both physically and mentally.

Patients also have the right to make decisions on the basis of informed consent, which allows them to make treatment decisions (either to give consent or to withhold consent) based on the information provided by their physicians. But, again, these decisions are based solely on the information, diagnosis, prognosis, and treatment course offered by the authority figure in the physician-patient relationship. This information may be selectively provided and filtered in order to obtain a particular decision. Patients are technically unsure the information is completely reliable or accurate. Often, patients may not even seek a second opinion for fear of angering the primary physician. In many cases, patients may be hesitant to question the physician's recommendations due to the authoritarian nature of the relationship. So informed consent is really consent given with a skewed or biased knowledge base.

Opponents of euthanasia and assisted suicide also regard the possibility that economic factors in institutional settings could influence and manipulate patients into selecting the option of death over other, more costly alternatives. With health care costs spiraling out of control, hospitals and other institutions (mental asylums, nursing homes, etc.) are seeking less expensive treatment alternatives and cost-cutting measures wherever feasible. It is not implausible to imagine that euthanasia and assisted suicide could provide an easily administered, inexpensive solution for the very expensive lingering maladies experienced by the terminally ill. Physicians, hospitals, and health maintenance organizations may lend support for euthanasia and assisted suicide to patients unable to pay for the treatment of a terminal illness or for those who are so hopelessly ill that treatment would most likely be unsuccessful when these resources could be utilized more productively on another patient with a higher chance of survival.

Insurance companies could further endorse the decisions of hospitals and physicians by limiting benefits for the terminally ill, restricting treatment options based on the official diagnosis and prognosis, and withdrawing palliative care and pain management assistance. It becomes less expensive for hospitals and insurance companies to assist patients in dying than to care for them throughout a hopeless, extended illness. Another aspect that must be considered in conjunction with these economic concerns and the legalization of euthanasia and assisted suicide is the fact that, in general, a large percentage of the money spent on health care in an individual's lifetime is expended in the last one to six months of life. The fact that euthanasia and assisted suicide regulations are directed at these particular situations pushes the economic issue to the forefront.

Economic factors must also be considered in terms of patients, their families, and society. Patients may have depleted their insurance benefits due to an extended illness, may have no insurance, may be a financial burden on their families (because of a depletion of insurance or lack of insurance), may have severe physical or mental handicaps, may be elderly and with a short life span remaining regardless of illness type, may be mentally incompetent and unable to rationally make a decision to die, or may belong to a socially stratified group (the poor, immigrants) that finds it difficult to obtain good medical care.[14] These patients become vulnerable to suggestions that euthanasia and assisted suicide are the best options. In a sense, a "duty to die" situation arises in which death becomes the seemingly best choice for all parties involved, and patients feel pressured into electing euthanasia or assisted suicide.

Patients who are feeling vulnerable because of their struggles with a terminal illness become very susceptible to pressures from family members and loved ones due to their extreme needs (both physically and emotionally). They do not want to become a burden on their families, be seen as weak, selfish, or irrational, and thus may be prone to accept any suggestions the family, loved ones, and the attending physician might make. At a time when they are most dependent on their close family for emotional support, respect, care, and strength, they may readily believe that they have an obligation to die because of the family's financial struggles and emotional suffering.[15] Unfortunately, economics could be a significant factor in a malevolent sense as well. If the family or spouse of the patient stands to gain a substantial inheritance, the motive for euthanasia or assisted suicide might not be based on purely merciful considerations. The rationale behind euthanasia and assisted suicide must be carefully weighed against the unspoken desires of the family for financial gain.

Finally, opponents state that euthanasia and assisted suicide would be administered in a framework of social inequality, discrimination, and prejudice. New York Ninth Circuit Court of Appeals Judge Robert Beezer, in a 1994 report conducted by the New York State Task Force on Life and Law, stated that "those who will be most vulnerable to abuse, error, or indifference are the poor, minorities, and those who are least educated and empowered. This risk does not reflect a judgment that physicians are more prejudiced or influenced by race or class than the rest of society—only that they are not exempt from the prejudices manifest in other areas of our collective life."[16] Opponents of euthanasia warn that those who are most easily disposed of will be taken advantage of.

Sanctity-of-Life Concerns

Equally important to opponents of euthanasia and assisted suicide as the slippery slope issues are religious ideations and other sanctity-of-life matters. In almost every religion, suicide is considered a crime against God, because the supreme power that grants life also determines when it should be terminated. The timing and manner of one's death is determined solely by God, so suicide is not a morally or ethically sanctioned option in any situation. The belief is that human life is a gift from God and should be highly regarded, irrespective of the circumstances of that life.[17] Existence in any capacity is thought to be superior to not living at all, as the human body is a conduit for spiritual reflection and moral contemplation. There is the additional contention that we hold a particular responsibility to our community, to other members of the community (especially the poor and disadvantaged), and to God for the life entrusted to us and that we must fulfill this commitment at any price.

In addition to these religious concerns, there is also the sentiment that human suffering has a positive, ennobling, redemptive value. Assisting others through the throes of illness instills in care providers a sense of altruism, benevolence, and charitableness. Patients benefit from the experience in another way. Christian patients, for instance, suffering the torments of a terminal illness, purportedly form closer spiritual and moral associations to the sufferings of the crucified Christ, as they are said to be experiencing the same kind of pain and agony Christ endured. While almost all religions are compassionate about the suffering of the terminally ill patient, many believe that the offering of proper medical treatment, companionship, love, protection, and prayer are preferred to interrupting life's natural course.[18]

Even though the Bible does not expressly condemn suicide, the Christian church has never sanctioned it. This position was made clear early in the history of the church. One of the earliest ecclesiastical scholars, St. Augustine, pronounced suicide to be in violation of the Sixth Commandment, "Thou shalt not kill."[19] Later interpretations of this lean toward a more liberal translation of not killing another human being (committing homicide). St. Thomas Aquinas held that suicide is a mortal sin and contrary to natural law, a completely selfish act that damages the entire community and appropriates God's authority on matters of life and death.[20]

Historically, the Roman Catholic Church has refused funeral rites and burial in consecrated ground to individuals who have committed suicide. These victims were relegated to other burial sites to serve as reminders of what becomes of those who violate church law.[21] Attitudes in modern times have shifted slightly, and some Catholic churches permit the interment of suicide victims in the church cemetery. This transition was precipitated by the complex social pressures and challenges confronting individuals today, which make it difficult for them to discern what is the morally acceptable path to follow and what are the proper decisions in a given situation.

Euthanasia and assisted suicide, like other contemporary social issues such as birth control, are subject to some controversy within the Catholic Church. The euthanasia debate was sparked in 1957 when Pope Pius XII addressed an international meeting of physicians on the question of prolonging life. The pope reiterated St. Thomas Aquinas's previously stated position and added that it is the patient who must choose whether the medical treatment is required and, further, that it is the patient who provides consent to the physician for treatment. In other words, the physician should follow the wishes of the patient. The responsibility of the patient's family lies in following the directives of the patient, if known, or what they feel the patient would consider ordinary means of treatment. The pope also stated that the physician can cease attempting to resuscitate the patient if it constitutes an unreasonable hardship or burden on the family.[22]

In 1970, Cardinal Jean Villot, addressing the International Federation of Catholic Medical Associations, asserted that physicians are not required to use all the medical technology available to resuscitate a patient in the final stages of a terminal illness. He stated that it was the physician's obligation to relieve the suffering but not, in all cases, to prolong life at all costs.[23] In 1980, the Vatican's Declaration on Euthanasia once again firmly established the Catholic Church's disapproval of euthanasia and assisted suicide. This position has been bolstered by assertions from Pope John Paul II.

But in recent years, this position has come under scrutiny. If physicians are interfering with divine providence by shortening life through euthanasia and assisted suicide, is not the converse true—that physicians are disturbing the divine order by prolonging life through medical technology and advances such as pacemakers, pharmaceuticals, organ transplants, and surgery?[24] If the argument is extended one step further to include pain management, then physicians are already obstructing God's plan. If pain and suffering serve a redemptive purpose, then should not the patient forgo anesthesia and painkillers? The Christian thinkers making these observations are not condemning all of Christian theological thinking; but they believe that the religious community is sometimes more concerned with religious doctrine than with the plight of real people and real situations in today's society and believe that certain ideologies are outdated.

As in the Catholic tradition, Judaism holds that only God has the power to grant and take away life. Every breath of human life up until the final extinguishing moment is held to be sacred, with existence in any state "superseding living the good life."[25] Within the Jewish tradition, the question of the acceptance or rejection of euthanasia and assisted suicide is framed slightly differently, but the interpretation results in answers to the same fundamental issues. In Judaism, abstract moral principles are usually converted into questions of legal obligation or responsibility. The inquiry is not whether an individual has a right to die, for example, or a right to an abortion, but rather what the individual is obliged to do. The questions that would be considered within a Jewish-perspective right-to-die debate are: What is a physician attending a terminally ill patient permitted to do in terms of precipitating death or stopping pain? If the physician assists the patient to die, is he or she legally liable? What is the terminally ill patient obliged to do?

Although the Talmud does not explicitly forbid suicide, there is a high level of agreement in the Orthodox Jewish tradition on the repudiation of active euthanasia and assisted-suicide practices. Perhaps this is due in part to the seemingly universal consensus on the subject among well-known works of literature by post-Talmudic scholars.[26] Within Jewish law, preservation of life is put above anything else, and accelerating death in any manner or being the direct cause of another's death is considered murder.[27] The noted exception to this is the act of martyrdom. In this case, sacrificing one's life is considered a duty. Controversy and confusion come from the meaning and translation of the phrase "direct cause." It is most often interpreted to mean that death must occur as a result of natural causes, not as a result of a direct action by the physician to prematurely end a life.

Passive euthanasia for a terminally ill patient is permitted under certain circumstances within the Jewish tradition. The Talmud implies that the physician does not have to do everything possible to keep the terminally ill patient alive. Removing artificial means that are keeping a patient from dying, such as a feeding tube, is not considered a positive or direct action, in that no element, such as a lethal dose of morphine, is introduced to cause death. The patient essentially dies from natural causes (for instance, starvation or dehydration), not from a positive action the physician undertook to induce death.[28] Under Jewish law, the physician or family does not have an obligation to pursue this path, but it is allowable under particular conditions. Thus, while there is an obligation to prolong natural life, there is no legal obligation to prolong life artificially.

Most Protestant denominations also oppose euthanasia and assisted suicide on similar grounds as the Catholic Church and the Jewish tradition. In 1988, however, the Unitarian Universalist Association advocated support for a right to self-determination in the dying process and freedom from prosecution for physicians who perform the procedure. Other churches have voiced support as well. The United Church of

Christ (Congregational) and the Methodist Church on the U.S. West Coast also support the principle of voluntary euthanasia.

The highly charged emotional issues of euthanasia and assisted suicide will continue to stir controversy for years to come. In a historical sense, the same key concepts that are in contention today have been subject to scrutiny by philosophers, theologians, medical professionals, and laypersons since ancient times.

3

Euthanasia in the United States and Canada

The United States

Citizens of the United States are entitled to certain fundamental rights guaranteed by the Constitution. Among these rights are the right to vote, the right to free speech, the right to bear arms, the right to worship any religion, the right to a trial by jury, the right to be secure from unreasonable search and seizures, and the right to peacefully assemble. These rights provide freedom of choice for the individual and the opportunity to control the direction and destiny of one's life. But the United States does not fully recognize the right of terminally ill patients to dictate the circumstances of their dying. Patients are denied the right to choose to die in a dignified, peaceful, and painless manner through voluntary euthanasia (via a lethal injection). In addition, in every state except Oregon, patients are further denied the right to choose death by physician-assisted suicide (via a lethal dose of medication prescribed by a physician). Terminally ill patients do have the right to die through the refusal of medical treatment. This may involve withdrawing a respirator and gradually suffocating to death, refusing food and slowly starving to death, or declining water and dying in approximately ten to twelve days.

In the twentieth century, a number of events have brought the modern right-to-die movement to its current status. The contemporary movement originated in two countries in the late 1930s. In 1935, the Voluntary Euthanasia Society was formed in Great Britain by Lord Moynihan and Dr. Killick Millard; in 1938, the Euthanasia Society of America was formed in the United States. In the following decades other concerns, such as World War II, eclipsed right-to-die concerns. By 1946, the Euthanasia Society of America had grown to over 500 members. In that same year, the Committee of 1776 Physicians for Legalizing Voluntary Euthanasia in New York State was formed.

By the late 1950s, significant medical and technological advances made it feasible to maintain terminally ill and permanently unconscious patients for a much longer period of time than previously possible, raising quality-of-life issues. Even though life could now be sustained longer, in light of lingering cancers and AIDS it was becoming questionable whether it was a life worth sustaining. For terminally ill patients, pain coupled with debilitating conditions gave rise to the concept of death with dignity. In 1967, Luis Kutner along with members of the Euthanasia Society of America developed the country's first living will and created the Euthanasia Education Council to disseminate this information to the public. The next year, Dr. Walter Sackett introduced the living will in Florida. By 1972, more than 100,000 living wills had been distributed in the United States.

In 1973, the American Hospital Association developed the Patient's Bill of Rights, which specifies patients' right to refuse treatment and right to informed consent. In 1974, a transition took place in the foremost right-to-die group. The Euthanasia Society of America changed its name to the Society for the Right to Die, and the Euthanasia Education Council became known as Concern for Dying. The 1976 New Jersey case of Karen Ann Quinlan was pivotal in energizing the right-to-die movement. This case essentially established the primacy of patients' wishes over the state's duty to preserve life. During that same year, California passed the California Natural Death Act, which was the first living-will statute to be enacted. A succession of treatment-refusal laws was passed by several states in 1977, followed by the recognition of advance directives by many others.

In 1980, another influential right-to-die organization, the Hemlock Society, formed. As right-to-die issues began to come to the forefront of social concerns, the Society for the Right to Die and Concern for Dying saw their membership skyrocket to nearly 70,000 by 1989. The following year, the U.S. Supreme Court found in the Nancy Cruzan case that the right to refuse medical treatment is guaranteed by the Constitution. Subsequent to this decision, the U.S. Congress passed the Patient Self-Determination Act, which was the first federal act to directly address the subject of advance directives. That same year, Dr. Jack Kevorkian began his crusade to assist individuals wishing to end their lives in a peaceful manner by helping Janet Adkins to end her life. In 1991, the Society for the Right to Die and Concern for Dying joined to form the group Choice in Dying. Right-to-die activist Derek Humphry published *Final Exit*, a compelling and controversial best-seller that provided guidance in ending one's life. Dr. Kevorkian was acquitted in 1994 of assisting in the suicide of Thomas Hyde and in 1996 was acquitted again in assisting in two other deaths.

In 1994, Oregon began its long battle to legalize physician-assisted suicide. Three years after its initial approval by voter referendum, voters again decided to retain the law to allow assisted suicide. This law permits physicians to prescribe a lethal dose of medication to terminally ill patients who request it. To obtain the medication, a minimum of two physicians must concur that the patient has less than six months to live. The case was tied up in appeals for three years, and in October 1997 the U.S. Supreme Court decided not to hear the case, thus clearing the way for the law to take effect. Technically, the law could have taken effect, but the referendum had been previously ordered by the state legislature. Now that legalization has occurred in one state, some experts and opinion leaders predict that the practice will spread to other states.[1] In fact, voters in Michigan may be able to decide for themselves in the fall of 1998 if they want the option of physician-assisted suicide. A grassroots group has collected the required signatures to put the issue on the November ballot, pending certification of the signatures. If a law passes, Michigan will be the second state to legalize physician-assisted suicide.[2]

The states of Washington and New York have been in legal battles regarding their bans on physician-assisted suicide. In Washington, the ban was declared unconstitutional in 1994 and was immediately appealed to the Ninth Circuit Court. In 1995, this court upheld the ban. The following year, the appeals court upheld the Ninth Circuit Court's decision and claimed that Washington's ban on physician-assisted suicide violated the liberty interest of the Fourteenth Amendment of the Constitution. The court's jurisdiction includes the states of Alaska, Arizona, California, Hawaii, Idaho, Montana, Nevada, Oregon, and Washington and the territory of Guam. In other words, that court's decision is precedent setting for all states within the court's jurisdiction. In the state of New York, patients and physicians brought a lawsuit against the state's ban on physician-assisted suicide in 1994. The court upheld the ban, and it was appealed to the Second Circuit Court. In 1996, the Second Circuit Court held that the ban on assisted suicide violated the equal protection clause of the Fourteenth Amendment. Both the Washington and the New York cases were appealed to the Supreme Court, which ruled that there was no constitutional right to physician-assisted suicide, thus leaving it up to the states to craft their own legislation.

Social Considerations

In 1900, one-third of all deaths occurred by the age of five, often causing parents to delay naming their children until they reached several years of age.[3] Those who survived the first five years looked forward to death from accidents, incurable disease, epidemics (such as influenza), poor nutrition, lack of medical knowledge, natural catastrophes (droughts and floods), childbirth, or hazardous living and working conditions. Another third of all deaths occurred before the age of fifty-five, and those remaining alive were considered old. By 1990, this trend had radically shifted, with 85 percent of the population in the United States dying after the age of fifty-five. As death has become less a part of everyday life, it has transitioned into something bordering on the unnatural and surreal.

A crucial indicator of the quality of life in a society is the overall health status of the general population, which is associated with the level of industrial development, the age and gender composition of the population, and the consequences of the stratification of wealth and power. Life expectancy has significantly increased in the twentieth century in the United States as well as in other industrialized nations of the world. In 1900, the average number of years an American was expected to live was forty-seven. By 1997, the average life expectancy had risen to seventy-six, with women averaging seven years longer than men. The increase in life expectancy is largely attributable to improvements in living and working conditions and to advances in medical technology. Social inequality is reflected in the difference in health among racial groups. For instance, African Americans, Mexican Americans, Puerto Ricans, and Native Americans have lower life expectancy rates than other Americans. Inferior health is the product of a complex array of factors, including overcrowded housing, lower incomes, jobs that do not have health care benefits, limited access to proper health care, and sanitation problems. Conversely, adequate income affords one access to the things that support a long, healthy life, such as nutritious foods, appropriate medical attention, and a safe living environment.

The United States does not have a national health care system available to all its citizens for a variety of reasons, including opposition to such a program by the American Medical Association and the health insurance industry, lack of political support, and the advocacy by Americans for limited government intrusion in the interest of greater personal liberty.[4] As a result, the United States has developed a health care system that is profit based—a direct-fee system. In this system, the patient is responsible for payment for all treatment or services rendered. Forms of payment for health care include personal financial resources or insurance coverage funded fully or partially through an employer or purchased privately at one's own expense. Obviously, those with higher incomes can afford to have better medical care than those who are less affluent.

The functioning of the health care system is also affected by the governmental system. The United States is a federal republic with a capitalist economy. The means of production (factories, knowledge, land, corporations) are privately owned and operated for the purpose of generating a profit for the owners. Theoretically, the interaction of supply and demand and competition among producers forces out less-efficient firms, leads to lower prices, and ultimately improves the well-being of society and its members. Free markets are said to exist within limits and are designed to ensure social stability. A significant problem with free enterprise is the reduction of competition via the concentration of wealth and economic power. This consolidation of wealth and power allows health insurance companies to decide who is eligible for coverage, what medical treatments will be paid for, what standards will be followed in terms of treatment or length of hospital stay, and what medications will be subsidized. Health insurance companies have become increasingly dictatorial, causing great concern among patients and the medical community.

Hospitals and physicians might support euthanasia for patients unable to pay for their treatment of a terminal illness or for those who are so hopelessly ill that treatment would likely be unsuccessful. Insurance companies could limit benefits for the terminally ill and instead assist them to die. Fears of this scenario arise from economically based decisions that are currently being made within the health care system.

Influential Case Histories

In the United States, approximately two million individuals a year die in a hospital, a nursing home, or a hospice.[5] Two out of three of these individuals die as a result of a chronic illness such as cancer or heart disease. Meanwhile President Bill Clinton's Commission for the Study of Ethical Problems in Medicine and Biomedical and Behavioral Research estimated that 5,000 patients are artificially kept alive in a permanently unconscious, vegetative state through either feeding tubes or ventilators. The case of Karen Ann Quinlan demonstrates the tension between legal regulations, the role of medicine and the medical community, and the desires of the patient's family.

The Cruzan case was technically the first right-to-die case that came before the U.S. Supreme Court. The constitutional question under consideration was whether Cruzan had the right to refuse treatment, as exercised by the authority of her parents, under the due process clause of the Fourteenth Amendment. The elevated evidentiary requirement that the parents produce clear and convincing evidence that their daughter would want her life support terminated was due to the fact that withdrawing treatment had irreversible consequences and the family might not necessarily act in the best interest of a member of the family deemed incompetent to make those decisions. The Court held that under the due process clause the state could require clear and convincing evidence that the patient would want the life-sustaining treatment terminated. The Court did not stipulate that the state must require such evidence, only that it was not unconstitutional to do so. They additionally stated that the parents had not produced the evidence that Cruzan would rather die than live in a persistent vegetative state. The protection of a patient's constitutional right to due process is paramount, even in situations in which the patient is deemed incompetent. Furthermore, the Supreme Court held that there was a constitutional right to refuse treatment. They also maintained that the state had arrogantly given itself the authority to define life and, as a result, left Cruzan's life in a state of flux.[6]

Cruzan's parents again initiated court proceedings, claiming that new witnesses could produce clear and convincing evidence of Cruzan's end-of-life wishes. The Missouri State Department of Health, which had originally opposed the parents' position, asked to be dismissed from the case and stated that it had no further interest and was ready to implement orders to withdraw nutrition and hydration. As a result of new testimony from Cruzan's former coworkers, the Circuit Court authorized the removal of her nutrition and hydration life-sustaining treatment. Cruzan died twelve days after ceasing treatment. This case led to the passage by Congress of the Patient Self-Determination Act, which serves to regulate living wills and durable powers of attorney and to require medical treatment providers to inform patients about their right to refuse medical and surgical treatment.[7]

A 1996 physician-assisted suicide case in Florida illustrates the frustration that terminally ill patients face when confronting the medical and legal systems. Charles Hall, who contracted AIDS through a blood transfusion in 1981, was suffering from hepatitis B, pneumonia, arthritis, a brain cyst, and partial, progressive blindness. Hall along with two other terminally ill patients (who have since died) and his physician sought the right to physician-assisted suicide in the state of Florida, where it has been banned since 1868. Their position was supported by both the Hemlock Society of Florida and the Palm Beach County chapter of the American Civil Liberties Union. The trial was held in Palm Beach County because that is where the physician who would have written the prescription for Hall resides. Circuit Court Judge Joseph Davis ruled in February 1997 that Hall did have a right to commit suicide with the help of his physician, Dr. Cecil McIver, who had agreed to write a prescription for a lethal dose of medication.

The right to physician-assisted suicide, Judge Davis said, is based on the privacy and equal protection clauses in the state and federal constitutions. A state constitutional amendment passed in 1980 provides for a stronger right of privacy than that of the federal constitution. The amendment states that individuals have the right to be free from governmental intrusion in their private lives.[8] Judge Davis also held that Dr. McIver could not have been legally prosecuted for his participation in Hall's death. The decision marked the first time in the United States that a judge officially supported physician-assisted suicide. Judge Davis's ruling implicitly stated that it applied only to Hall and only in Palm Beach County.

The state appealed the ruling within two hours, and the decision was automatically stayed. The appeal was based on the position that physician-assisted suicide is considered manslaughter in the state of Florida.[9] Circuit Judge Lucy Brown then lifted the stay, and the Fourth District Court of Appeals requested that the Florida Supreme Court accept the case. Judge Brown believed that if the stay were not lifted, Hall would be denied the right to die in a dignified and comfortable manner because of the lengthy appeals process. Assistant Attorney General Charles Fahlbusch requested an emergency hearing to reinstate the stay on the premise that the act of physician-assisted suicide is irreversible should the higher court reverse the district court's ruling. The Florida Supreme Court immediately reinstated the stay and agreed to hear the case in May.

The Florida Board of Medicine announced that they would not allow physician-assisted suicide and that Dr. McIver would sanctions from the Board, including losing his license to practice medicine, if he helped Hall commit suicide.[10] Another case was initiated to prevent the Florida board of Medicine from investigating and punishing Dr. McIver, but in 1996, the board had already agreed not to find Dr. McIver in violation of practice standards if Hall wanted assistance in dying. As a result of a court order, the agreement still remained valid. The Florida Supreme Court overturned the lower court's ruling that assisted suicide should be allowed under the privacy provision of Florida's constitution. One of the court's chief concerns was preventing the integrity of the medical profession from deteriorating. The court's ruling does not prevent the state legislature from enacting a physician-assisted suicide law in the future. Hall died in March 1998 surrounded by family and friends.

Right-to-Die Organizations

Several right-to-die groups have sprung into existence in the twentieth century in the United States. Many of these nonprofit groups have been influential in making death and dying issues a priority concern for a rapidly aging population. Right-to-die societies saw tremendous growth in their membership rolls as the first baby boomers began to reach their fifties. From 1960 until 1994, the total population in the United States increased 45 percent, while the segment eighty-five years and older increased a dramatic 247 percent. This is now the most rapidly increasing group within the population. The eighty-five and older age group was composed of nearly four million individuals in 1996 and is expected to increase to between nine million and thirty million by 2050. It has been estimated that individuals older than sixty-five will represent between one-fifth and one-fourth of the total population at that time.[11]

These shifts in the age of the population will have a significant impact on health care, training of medical personnel, and social policy developments. The greatest concerns Americans express about growing old include being confined to a nursing home for an extended period of time, developing Alzheimer's disease, and becoming a financial burden on others. Of those individuals age seventy and older, 80 percent report having a major chronic disease, 36 percent describe themselves as frail and in need of assistance in functioning, and 36 percent say they have cognitive problems. Only 16 percent stated they are in overall excellent health.[12] When asked specifically about their greatest fear associated with dying, respondents in another survey cited being a burden to their family and friends (40 percent), fear of pain (14 percent), lack of control (8 percent), and losing dignity (8 percent). Right-to-die societies offer a form of security and reassurance to the aging population worried about end-of-life issues.[13]

The Hemlock Society USA, a grassroots organization formed in 1980, now boasts over 25,000 members. The demographic composition of the group membership is somewhat contrary to the national statistics of typical euthanasia supporters in the United States. Nearly two-thirds of the society's members are female, although surveys conducted on euthanasia demographics reveal that female support for right-to-die issues is less than that of males across all age categories. With respect to religious denominations of members, the group is highly overrepresented in the categories of no religious affiliation and Jewish affiliation. The median age of a Hemlock Society member is between sixty-five and seventy-four years. The group is composed almost entirely of Caucasians; however, Native Americans compose a greater percentage than their proportion in the national population. As a whole, the members have attained educational levels that far surpass that of the general population and report an average household income of $50,000. The group is politically active: nearly 50 percent consider themselves Democrats,

24 percent identify themselves as independents, and almost 22 percent self-report as Republicans.[14] The Hemlock Society supports legalized physician-assisted dying for terminally ill adults and is an advocate for patient's rights and for assisting individuals with making informed choices and empowering them through greater knowledge. Their primary goals are to increase public awareness of right-to-die issues and to effect change in public policies.

In 1993, the Patients' Rights Organization—USA was formed as a social welfare affiliate. Since its founding the group has been politically active in advancing the right-to-die cause. Choice in Dying, a nonprofit group, advocates the right of patients to be involved in decisions about medical treatment at or near the end of life and seeks to assist terminally ill patients and their loved ones. Choice in Dying pioneered the living will almost three decades ago and has since distributed approximately ten million copies. The group provides many services to the terminally ill patient and the general public. Through an extensive education campaign it hopes to teach health care professionals as well as the general pubic about end-of-life concerns and the benefits of advance directives. In addition, it provides forums for public debates on right-to-die issues. In conjunction with this program, Choice in Dying also prepares and develops publications for both professionals involved in the field and the general public. On the political front, the group is active in attempting to improve upon nonexistent or current regulations regarding dying in the United States. It also works with health care facilities to better educate them about advance directives, end-of-life decision making, and pain care.

Pain Management

The fear of death in the United States is generally resolved by the individual in one of two ways. In the first way, individuals deny the possibility of death and assault it with all the modern medical technology possible. The second method is to head off a painful death through physician-assisted suicide. Fearing a painful, lingering death, many individuals have a backup plan in case things do not go as planned. A 1997 survey supported this fear, revealing that 50 percent of hospital patients experiencing substantial pain were never questioned by their physician about how much they hurt.[15] Another study, conducted by a group of physicians, showed that patients do not clearly communicate their wishes to their medical care providers. For example, just over 20 percent of the patients expressed their desires regarding cardiopulmonary resuscitation with their physicians, and of those patients who had not discussed it with their physician, almost 60 percent did not have plans to do so.[16] Many opponents of euthanasia and physician-assisted suicide believe that the right-to-die movement is in reality a cry for help in the areas of pain management and health care reform. In other words, the question of physician-assisted suicide would never arise if society did a better job of taking care of individuals at the end of their lives.[17] They believe that patients do not really want to kill themselves: they are simply seeking relief from suffering.

According to a study conducted by Dartmouth Medical School, the care individuals receive in the final stages of a terminal illness is greatly influenced by where they live and the distribution of medical care facilities and medical personnel.[18] The study found that individuals who reside in the eastern part of the United States (especially in the cities of New York and Miami) are more likely to die in hospitals than those in any other areas, and there is a five-times greater chance that these patients will also be attached to some type of medical equipment (respirator, feeding device, etc.) for a period of time during the last six months of life in the intensive care unit, even though they are no more ill than those in other regions of the United States. The amount of medical treatment received at the end of life appears to be significantly correlated with the distribution of services and facilities as well. Where there are more hospital beds and physicians, there are more patients' occupying the beds.[19] Finally, the study reveals that patients medical treatment preferences are unrelated to the amount they receive. The study's authors believe that the characteristics of the health care system in the area where the patient resides govern how much treatment patients will receive. What patients desire or what is best for them are less influential.

Another issue involves hospice care. Only 17 percent of all dying patients receive hospice care.[20] Many complications and difficulties arise when the patient attempts to gain access to such care. First, to arrange for the transition to a hospice care treatment facility, the physician must discuss the arrangements with the patient. In many instances, the physician will find this difficult to do as it might be seen as giving up and serve to take away hope of recovery in the mind of the patient. Another factor that makes the transition to hospice care difficult lies in accurately predicting the remaining time a patient is expected to live. This task may be easier with such diseases as cancer and more complicated in cases of Alzheimer's disease. Thus, if a misjudgment is made by the physician, there may not be enough time left to make preparations for the transition to a hospice care facility.

Another problem is providing home care in conjunction with hospice care. Many hospice programs emphasize home care, but this is not possible for many patients because they either live alone or have no family members who can attend to their needs on a full-time basis. In addition, many private insurance companies do not fully cover hospice care for many illnesses, thus limiting this option for pain treatment for the patient. Patients in this situation are forced to choose between continuing aggressive treatment they no longer desire or going without treatment entirely.[21] Most euthanasia and physician-assisted suicide advocates support hospice treatment, but not every patient wants to be tranquilized into a subconscious state, and, further, pain treatment is not always effective.[22] Euthanasia and physician-assisted suicide should be the last options, when pain is neither controllable nor tolerable.

Instead of simply calculating life expectancy statistics, perhaps the medical community ought to rely on DALE numbers. DALE is an acronym for disability-adjusted life expectancy and numerically estimates the effects of a disabling illness, a fatal disease, and injuries to arrive at one's health expectancy. The point of determining an individual's DALE is not to predict how long one will live but rather how long one will live well. This number takes into consideration the burden of an illness or injury on the individual.[23]

Public Opinion Data

Since the establishment of the Euthanasia Society of America in 1938, support for physician-assisted suicide has been steadily growing. In 1947, 37 percent of Americans said yes to the question, When a person has a disease that cannot be cured, do you think doctors should be allowed by law to end the patient's life if the patient and his or her family request it? By 1973, 53 percent agreed, and by 1982, 61 percent agreed.[24] In 1994, a survey was conducted of 1,307 Michigan adults, asking them to choose between a law banning all physician-assisted suicide and a law that would allow it with specified criteria and safeguards: 66 percent supported legalization and 26 percent preferred the ban. To the question, Try to imagine that doctors discovered that you have a terminal illness that is certain to involve a great deal of pain and suffering. If physician-assisted suicide were legally available do you think you might request it for yourself? 24 percent replied yes, definitely; 24 percent said probably; 22 percent were uncertain; 9 percent said probably not, and 21 percent said definitely not. A USA Today/CNN/Gallup poll conducted in April 1996 reported that 75 percent of Americans favored physician-assisted suicide, while only 22 percent were opposed to it.[25]

In May 1997 another national survey reported an 80 percent positive reply to the question, Should doctors help their patients commit suicide? Eighty-one percent said they would support a family member's decision to commit suicide if that person were terminally ill. The study posed two additional questions. When asked, How persuasive do you find the argument that a terminally ill patient has the right to die with dignity and should be able to ask for help to commit suicide? 73 percent said the argument was very persuasive, and only 14 percent said it was not persuasive at all. The second question read, How persuasive do you find the argument that physician-assisted suicide is wrong because all life is sacred? Nearly 50 percent replied that the argument was not at all persuasive, and 23 percent said it was not very persuasive, 11 percent said it was somewhat persuasive, and 18 percent said it was very persuasive.[26]

In 1988, the Center for Health Ethics and Policy at the University of Colorado, Graduate School of Public Affairs, surveyed all Colorado physicians and found that 35 percent of them had given patients pain medication that had the effect of shortening the patients' lives (whether intended or not); while 60 percent cared for patients for whom they believed active euthanasia would be justified. Further, 35 percent said they would be willing to administer a lethal dose if it were legal to do so, and 4 percent said they had helped patients to stockpile a lethal dose of medication for the purpose of suicide.[27] A 1995 survey of Oregon physicians inquired about their beliefs on assisted suicide: 60 percent felt that it should be legal in some cases, 66 percent said it would be ethical in some cases, 33 percent stated that it would be immoral, 34 percent said it would violate their professional ethics, and 30 percent said it would violate their personal beliefs.[28]

A similar survey was administered to Michigan physicians in 1994 and 1995. The physicians were asked if they would be likely to participate in a suicide if a patient requested it, if it were legal, and if all the legal guidelines were met; 22 percent responded that they might be willing to participate, with either the patient or the physician taking the final action, and 13 percent said they would be willing to participate but only if "the patient takes the final action."[29] In a recent study, 56 percent said they favored allowing a physician to assist a patient to commit suicide, and 35 percent stated that if it were legal they "might offer" to help.[30] A 1995 study of Washington physicians concluded that requests for assistance with suicide is not uncommon. In 1994, one out of every six physicians in the state reported receiving a request for physician-assisted suicide. By 1995, that figure had increased to one out of every four.[31]

Many studies have been undertaken in the United States examining basic demographics associated with various aspects of right-to-die issues. With regard to age of people who support euthanasia, there has been much controversy as to whether individuals become more or less supportive of euthanasia as they grow older. Data support both arguments.[32] In his research, Raymond Leinbach stated that older individuals generally do not become less supportive of euthanasia as they age; and that any attitudinal change is very slight. On the other hand, Larry Seidlitz stated that older individuals are not highly accepting of physician-assisted suicide, noting that only 41 percent of his sample approved. Other factors, such as religious beliefs, have also been tested. Anne Jordan reported that religious influences prevail over attitudes toward euthanasia issues. With respect to euthanasia when an incurable illness is present (as opposed to simply psychological distress), religion and confidence in the federal government were most important in predicting attitudes about voluntary death issues.[33]

A telephone survey in 1996 reported some basic demographic characteristics of individuals who answered the question, Should it be legal or illegal for a doctor to help a terminally ill patient commit suicide? Fifty-one percent of the persons surveyed supported the legalization of physician-assisted suicide; 40 percent were opposed. Overall, more men (54 percent) than women (47 percent) favored the legalization of physician-assisted suicide; 37 percent of the men and 44 percent of the women were against legalization. When examined by race, 70 percent of African Americans opposed legalization; 20 percent favored it. Conversely, Caucasians were more likely to support physician-assisted suicide: 55 percent supported legalization, while 35 percent opposed it. Respondents under the age of fifty-nine supported legalization by at least a 50 percent majority. Respondents over seventy years old were least likely to support it. The more educated and the more affluent respondents were likely to favor it. Respondents in the over-$75,000 income bracket showed the greatest support.[34] A survey conducted in 1997 supports these results. It found that respondents who were most likely to support maintaining life regardless of the circumstances were African Americans who had lower incomes and placed great importance on religion.[35]

The Current Legal Status and the Supreme Court Decision

Assisted suicide is criminalized by statute in thirty-six states, and in eight states it is criminalized by common law. Advance directives and living-will legislation vary by state. Advance directives generally refer to patients' oral or written instructions concerning their future medical care in the event they are incapable of speaking for themselves. Advance directives usually take the form of a living will or a medical power of attorney. Living wills express individuals' desires in writing about the medical treatment they wish to receive in the future should they be physically unable to communicate. A medical power of attorney allows individuals to appoint someone to make medical decisions for them should they not be able to make those decisions for themselves. Table 3.1 reports such legislation by state as of July 1997.

Even with a majority of the general population supporting the right-to-die agenda, there has been significant opposition from various factions in the United States, and the issues have been deeply divisive of the general public and the medical community.[36] In the last two decades, progress on right-to-die issues has been slower than one might expect considering the high level of public approval. On October 1, 1996, the Supreme Court agreed to hear the cases from Washington and New York in order to determine if the Constitution provides a terminally ill patient a right to the assistance of a physician in hastening death.[37] The Court heard appeals from the states of Washington and New York, where it was earlier determined that a terminally ill patient who is mentally competent has a constitutional right to physician-assisted suicide. These states attempted to sustain their existing laws, which have been on the books since the nineteenth century, that make it illegal for anyone (including a physician) to assist someone to commit suicide. In *Compassion in Dying v. Washington*, the Ninth United States Circuit Court held that the patient has a privacy right to assisted suicide under the Constitution's guarantee of due process. In *Quill v. Vacco*, the Second Circuit Court of New York held that terminally ill patients have the right to hasten death through the use of drugs, just as other patients have the right to refuse artificial life supports under the Constitution's equal protection guarantee.[38]

Friend of the court (amicus curiae) briefs were filed by a broad array of individuals and groups, including theologians, philosophers, politicians, the medical community, groups representing the disabled and the chronically ill, women's organizations, Planned Parenthood, and the Clinton administration. The briefs strongly urged the Court to declare that the states have the constitutional right to ban physician-assisted suicide. In January 1997, the Court listened for two hours to arguments from both sides. The justices went beyond the traditional legal questions and considered moral implications, medical technology, social attitudes, and even their own personal experiences with the dying process. After the questioning session, it seemed evident that a majority of the justices would not find a constitutional right to physician-assisted suicide.[39] Indeed, on June 26, 1997, the justices declared in a unanimous decision that there was no constitutional guarantee to physician-assisted suicide, thus leaving in place both New York and Washington States' bans on the practice. Physician-assisted suicide was not found to be unconstitutional. Instead the ruling left the issue to be resolved at the state level through the legislature or ballot box.[40]

Table 3.1 Status of Right-to-Die Legislation in the United States, by State, July 1997

State	*Physician-Assisted Suicide*	*Living Will*	*Health Care Agent*	*Other Legislation*
Alabama	Criminalized by common law	Yes	Yes	H553 amends the Natural Death Act and expands circumstances under which life-sustaining treatment may be refused in a living will.
Alaska	Criminalized by statute	Yes	No	538 authorizes an individual to provide an anatomical gift in a declaration. It also provides for procedures regarding do-not-resuscitate orders when an anatomical gift is to be made upon a person's death.
Arizona	Criminalized by statute	Yes	Yes	Not applicable.
Arkansas	Criminalized by statute	Yes	Yes	Not applicable.

Table 3.1—Continued

State	*Physician-Assisted Suicide*	*Living Will*	*Health Care Agent*	*Other Legislation*
California	Criminalized by state	Yes	Yes	AB3171 stipulates that the Division of Licensing of the Medical Board of California will consider a course regarding the special needs of individuals confronting end-of-life issues.
Colorado	Criminalized by statute	Yes	Yes	HB1013 permits pharmacies to dispense certain controlled substances without obtaining written authorization from a physician in emergencies involving hospice patients.
Connecticut	Criminalized by statute	Yes	Yes	HB5216 establishes nonhospital and inpatient do-not-resuscitate law.
Delaware	Criminalized by statute	Yes	Yes	SB408 adds provisions governing non-hospital do-not-resuscitate orders to the Natural Death Act.
Florida	Criminalized by common law	Yes	Yes	Not applicable.
Georgia	Criminalized by statute in certain limited circumstances	Yes	Yes	SB35 amends existing do-not-resuscitate laws clarifying non-hospital provisions.

Hawaii	Criminalized by statute	Yes	Yes	Not applicable.
Idaho	Criminalized by common law	Yes	Yes	Not applicable.
Illinois	Criminalized by statute	Yes	Yes	Not applicable.
Indiana	Criminalized by statute	Yes	Yes	Not applicable.
Iowa	Criminalized by statute	Yes	Yes	SB2066 makes physician-assisted suicide a Class C felony.
Kansas	Criminalized by statute	Yes	Yes	Not applicable.
Kentucky	Criminalized by statute	Yes	Yes	Not applicable.
Louisiana	Criminalized by statute	Yes	Yes	H2492 permits the prescribing/administering of controlled dangerous substances by a physician for intractable pain.
Maine	Criminalized by statute	Yes	Yes	HB3182 creates the Uniform Health Care Decisions Act.
Massachusetts	Criminalized by common law	No	Yes	Not applicable.

Table 3.1—continued

State	*Physician-Assisted Suicide*	*Living Will*	*Health Care Agent*	*Other Legislation*
Michigan	Criminalized by common law	No	Yes	SB1102 established the Michigan Dignified Death Act, which sets procedures for informing terminally ill patients about treatment options and alternatives.
Minnesota	Criminalized by statute	Yes	Yes	HB179 allows advance directives to be listed on driver's license.
Mississippi	Criminalized by statute	Yes	Yes	Not applicable.
Missouri	Criminalized by statute	Yes	Yes	Not applicable.
Montana	Criminalized by statute	Yes	Yes	Not applicable.
Nebraska	Criminalized by statute	Yes	Yes	Not applicable.
Nevada	Criminalized by common law	Yes	Yes	Not applicable.
New Hampshire	Criminalized by statute	Yes	Yes	Not applicable.
New Jersey	Criminalized by statute	Yes	Yes	Not applicable.
New Mexico	Criminalized by statute	Yes	Yes	H1202 sets guidelines for advance health care directives.

New York	Criminalized by statute	No	Yes	Not applicable.
North Carolina	Criminalized by statute	Yes	Yes	Not applicable.
North Dakota	Criminalized by statute	Yes	Yes	Not applicable.
Ohio	Law is vague	Yes	Yes	H187 grants the authority to physicians to prescribe/dispense/administer controlled substances for pain management.
Oklahoma	Criminalized by statute	Yes	Yes	Not applicable.
Oregon	Legalized by referendum	Yes	Yes	SB1026 adds an organ donation section to the Health Care Decisions Act.
Pennsylvania	Criminalized by statute	Yes	Yes	Not applicable.
Rhode Island	Criminalized by statute	Yes	Yes	S836 prohibits a physician from being subject to disciplinary action solely for prescribing/administering/dispensing controlled substances for intractable pain.
South Carolina	Criminalized by statute	Yes	Yes	Not applicable.
South Dakota	Criminalized by statute	Yes	Yes	SB196 calls for civil enforcement of assisted-suicide statutes.

Table 3.1—Continued

State	*Physician-Assisted Suicide*	*Living Will*	*Health Care Agent*	*Other Legislation*
Tennessee	Criiminalized by statute	Yes	Yes	SB2743 amends law governing non-hospital do-not-resuscitate orders.
Texas	Criminalized by statute	Yes	Yes	Non applicable.
Utah	Law is vague	Yes	Yes	Non applicable.
Vermont	Criminalized by common law	Yes	Yes	Non applicable.
Virginia	Law is vague	Yes	Yes	SB788 provides for civil penalties and remedies relating to assisting a suicide.
Washington	Criminalized by statute	Yes	Yes	Non applicable.
West Virginia	Criminalized by common law	Yes	Yes	Non applicable.
Wisconsin	Criminalized by common law	Yes	Yes	SB658 amends the Natural Death Act, adding clauses governing nonhospital do-not-resuscitate orders.
Wyoming	Law is vague	Yes	Yes	Non applicable.

In Summary

The current status of euthanasia and physician-assisted suicide rights and regulations in the United States is a result of an intricate and unique evolution of the dying process in the twentieth century, a rapidly increasing segment of the population over sixty-five, incredible advancements in medical technology, the existence of a fee-based health insurance system operating in a capitalist economy, and the influence of religious groups. The fact that the United States is a federal republic also adds to the equation. Traditionally, a republic is founded on the principles of elected representation and democratic control by the citizenry, which allows for substantial citizen influence in generating and crafting social policy. Thus, it is a system in which the majority opinion dominates and is capable of influencing key political decision makers. The individual states will be the next battlefront for the euthanasia debate, as the Supreme Court did not find the right to physician-assisted suicide to be a guarantee originally penned in the Constitution. Confrontation at the state level will be interesting, contentious, and intriguing due to the vastly divergent demographic compositions of the states, coupled with the emergence of the new power generation—senior citizens.

Canada

While suicide is legal in Canada, neither euthanasia nor physician-assisted suicide are legally sanctioned options for terminating one's life.[41] Three sections of Canada's *Criminal Code* are germane to the euthanasia and physician-assisted suicide debate: Sections 14, 241, and 215. Section 14 applies directly to cases of euthanasia, stating that "no person is entitled to consent to have death inflicted on him, and such consent does not affect the criminal responsibility of any person by whom death may be inflicted on the person by whom consent is given." Section 241 makes assisting suicide in any capacity criminal. It states, "Everyone who counsels a person to commit suicide or aids or abets a person to commit suicide, whether suicide ensues or not, is guilty of an indictable offense and liable to imprisonment for a term not exceeding fourteen years." Section 215 is directed at preventing physicians from withholding or withdrawing life-sustaining treatments for euthanasia purposes. Section 215 holds that "everyone is under a legal duty to provide necessaries of life to a person under his charge if that person is unable, by reason of . . . illness, mental disorder or other cause, to withdraw himself from that charge and is unable to provide himself with the necessaries of life." Further extending this protection of the individual, physicians are obligated to ensure that patients deemed suicidal are prevented from harming themselves. But under Canada's *Charter of Rights and Freedoms* individuals do maintain basic rights to refuse medical treatment and to decide what medical treatment to pursue or decline, even if this rejection of treatment or care leads to their death.

Social Considerations

Some twenty-nine million Canadian citizens have access to free medical health care, with the exception of dental services. Once Canadians reach the age of sixty-five, the majority of their prescription drugs are free, as well. In a sense, the government acts like a large insurance company in that it is directly responsible for reimbursing physicians and hospitals, which operate privately. The federal government, in cooperation with the provincial governments, establishes a schedule of fees for medical services throughout the country. Thus, Canada's health system is not true socialized medicine since it is regulated and funded by the government but medical practitioners operate privately. Some physicians do successfully operate completely outside of this network, setting their own fee schedules.

While Canada is able to provide health care for all its citizens at a lower cost than is feasible in the United States, its medical system is frequently backlogged; individuals often wait months or years for surgical procedures, and state-of-the-art technology is not as widely used and applied.[42] Canada also provides a broad range of social services that serve as a safety net for the general population. The country's extensive social security system provides and funds old-age pensions, welfare, unemployment insurance, and a family allowance. In part because of Canada's comprehensive social services, the average life span for a Canadian is just over seventy-seven years of age. Because the health care system is publicly funded, no obvious economic motivations exist for the medical community or the patient's family to support euthanasia or physician-assisted suicide. The state, as provider of the funds that support the program, could also seek to trim its costs, but since Canada does not suffer from an economic crisis, a population explosion, or overcrowding, it also lacks any motive.

Legislative Statutes and Appellate Court Decisions

The Special Senate Committee on Euthanasia and Assisted Suicide was formed in 1994 after a highly publicized effort by Sue Rodriguez to legalize euthanasia was narrowly defeated by the Canadian Supreme Court. Rodriguez, who was suffering from amyotrophic lateral sclerosis (Lou Gehrig's disease), defied the Court ruling and eventually committed suicide with the assistance of an unnamed physician. The committee studied the legal, social, and ethical issues surrounding euthanasia and assisted suicide to enable the introduction of a bill on which there would have been a free vote by members of the Canadian Parliament. The committee listened to extremely emotional testimony from hundreds of Canadians, including medical experts, lawyers, ethicists, and ordinary citizens who had witnessed relatives or spouses die painfully from lingering illnesses.

In 1995, the committee issued its report and recommended against the legalization of both euthanasia and assisted suicide. It made recommendations in several areas, including palliative care, pain-control and sedation practices, withholding and withdrawing life-sustaining treatment, advance directives, assisted suicide, and euthanasia. The committee suggested that palliative care programs become a top priority during the restructuring of the national health care system. In addition, it urged the continued development and implementation of guidelines and standards. With respect to pain control and pain management, the committee recommended that the *Criminal Code* be revised to elucidate the practice of providing medical treatment for the purpose of relieving pain that may have the effect of shortening the patient's life. It further suggested that education and training in pain control and pain management be expanded and improved in the medical community.

The committee also agreed that the *Criminal Code* be modified to allow terminally ill individuals or their surrogates the right to withhold or withdraw life-sustaining treatment in certain circumstances. The circumstances under which this would be permitted are to be clarified in a set of national guidelines. The committee further concluded that in cases involving voluntary or nonvoluntary euthanasia, the judge does not necessarily have to mete out a harsh sentence when a more lenient one would be appropriate. The elements of compassion and mercy would, of course, be requisite to warrant this treatment. One possible method of delivering a more lenient sentence would be to implement a third category of murder: compassionate homicide. This crime would not carry the traditional mandatory life sentence but a less severe one.[43] No legislation has yet been approved as a result of the committee's study.

Influential Case Histories

Several cases in the Canadian courts paved the way for establishing some patients' rights in making decisions regarding their medical treatment at the end of life. One of the most noted cases is that of Sue Rodriguez. In 1981, Rodriguez developed the symptoms of a degenerative condition of her nervous system that ultimately results in full loss of all muscle function, including swallowing and breathing. A year later, she began her battle to change the existing *Criminal Code* to legalize assisted suicide. The battle culminated in 1993 when the Canadian Supreme Court handed down a narrow defeat against Rodriguez in a five-to-four decision. Four months after the decision, Rodriguez committed suicide with the assistance of an anonymous physician in the presence of Svend Robinson, a member of the Canadian Parliament. Robinson had been a key supporter and friend during Rodriguez's fight for legalization. Robinson was not prosecuted for his role in her death as there was not enough evidence to press charges, and he was protected by his constitutional right to remain silent. As a result of the intense publicity and interest generated by the case, a committee was formed to investigate in depth the issue of euthanasia and assisted suicide.[44]

The most sensational case to come to light is that of Dr. Nancy Morrison. Dr. Morrison was charged with first-degree murder in June 1997 in the death of her patient Paul Mills. In the last six months of his life, Mills had undergone ten operations to relieve his throat cancer. He was experiencing excruciating pain and incredible discomfort from the side effects of the cancer. His family eventually requested that all life-support treatment be withdrawn. Mills was said to be within hours of his death when this decision was made. At this juncture, Dr. Morrison administered an injection of potassium chloride without consulting Mills's family. Potassium chloride can have the double effect of being therapeutic and causing death by stopping the heart from beating. Mills died shortly after the injection was given. His death was listed on his medical records as precipitated by natural causes relating to his infections. After an internal review by the hospital, Dr. Morrison was relieved of her duties in the intensive care unit for three months. A colleague who believed the punishment to be inadequate contacted the police about the incident.

On two other occasions in Canada, medical professionals have been charged with murder for using potassium chloride on their terminally ill patients, but the prosecutors ultimately reduced the charges to the much less serious offense of administering a noxious substance. The Mills case had the potential to push Canadian lawmakers to clarify the country's legal stance on the administration of pain medication for the terminally ill as well as on other hazy issues surrounding euthanasia and physician-assisted suicide. The case was expected to go to trial in 1998.[45] In late February 1998 a provincial court judge ruled that there was not enough evidence to send the case to trial for murder or for any lesser charge.[46] Several senators have called for guidelines regarding withholding treatment from dying patients.

Public Opinion Data

The Canadian public has expressed strong support for the right to die. A study conducted in 1995 found that 85 percent of the respondents approved of a decision to halt life-sustaining treatment for a competent patient unlikely to recover; 66 percent approved of euthanasia for a competent patient unlikely to recover; and 55 percent approved of assisted suicide. In the situation of an incompetent patient unlikely to recover, 88 percent agreed to the termination of life-sustaining treatment if the patient had previously expressed such wishes through a living will; 76 percent approved of removing such treatment from an incompetent patient based upon a family request; only 35 percent approved of forgoing life-sustaining treatment when the patient was likely to recover.[47]

Gallup Canada Inc. and *Dying with Dignity, Canada,* have together conducted polls on euthanasia and assisted suicide since 1968. After the Special Senate Committee on Euthanasia and Assisted Suicide published its results in 1995, they conducted another poll with some of the questions revised in an attempt to reflect the contemporary state of events. The poll further sought to explore reactions to a situation in which an individual was chronically ill (as opposed to terminally ill) but nonetheless suffering from irreversible conditions with no chance of recovery. The question involving immediate life-threatening cases asked, When a person has an incurable disease that is immediately life threatening and causes that person to experience great suffering, do you, or do you not, think that competent doctors should be allowed by law to end the patient's life through mercy killing, if the patient has made a formal request in writing? Seventy-five percent supported the view that the physician should be allowed to terminate the life of the patient in this situation; 17 percent believed this should not be permitted; 8 percent had no opinion. The question regarding a nonimmediate life-threatening situation asked, When a person has an incurable disease that is not immediately life threatening but causes that person to experience great suffering, do you, or do you not, think that competent doctors should be allowed by law to end the patient's life through mercy killing, if the patient has made a formal request in writing? Overall, Canadians were not as supportive of this position. Only 57 percent favored mercy killing; 32 percent did not find mercy killing acceptable for the suffering chronically ill; 11 percent had no opinion.[48]

Current Legal Status

Canada's legal stance on euthanasia and physician-assisted suicide has been in a stalled position since the recommendations of the Special

Senate Committee on Euthanasia and Assisted Suicide were released in 1995. No new legislation has been created as a result of these comprehensive hearings and extensive studies. With the case of Dr. Nancy Morrison on the horizon, at the bare minimum Canada may be pushed to implement legislation defining the double effect of pain medication for the terminally ill patient.

Proponents of euthanasia in Canada believe that the *Criminal Code* effectively denies the individual the right of self-determination in choosing the circumstances of one's own death.[49] In fact, in some instances the *Criminal Code* seems to work directly against the right of self-determination. This is particularly true of Sections 14, 241, and 217. Section 14 effectively states that active support in any manner in the act of suicide or counseling an individual about suicide is against the law, while Section 241 prevents anyone from assisting in another person's death. Section 217 mandates that everyone has a legal duty to act wherever a failure to do so would result in a danger to life. The codes are presented in such a way as to require individuals to act to preserve life or to prevent the death of another individual, regardless of that individual's wish to live or die. Together, these codes have the effect of prohibiting self-determination in the matter of one's own death.

4

Euthanasia in the Netherlands, the United Kingdom, Germany, Switzerland, Spain, and France

The Netherlands

Social Considerations

The development of the current euthanasia and physician-assisted suicide policies in the Netherlands stems from that country's unique manner of understanding contemporary social problems and its creative approaches to their resolution. In the Netherlands, the guiding moral principle behind the practice of euthanasia can best be characterized as self-determination, or individual autonomy. This is consistent with the notion of social individualism in an industrialized society. Industrialization tends to decrease social inequality and increase the standard of living for the underprivileged poor. Technical work in an industrialized nation, which requires training and advanced skills, increases the demand for education and in turn decreases illiteracy and improves other social skills.

Another factor contributing to the uniqueness of the social position on euthanasia and physician-assisted suicide in the Netherlands lies in the medical community and the health care system. The Netherlands has one of the highest health and medical standards in the world. With one of the longest predicted life spans in the world for both men and women, it is not surprising that more than 99 percent of the citizens are covered by health insurance and that everyone is insured for the expense of any protracted illness.[1] Thus, no financial incentives exist for the medical community or the family to cease or reduce treatment and benefits for a patient. The government-guaranteed health care system allows for a long-term relationship to develop between patient and physician.

The majority of primary-care treatment is provided by general practitioners who reside in the community of the patients they treat and make house calls when patients are too ill to visit their offices.[2] Physicians get to know their patients' families and lifestyles over the course of treatment. Moreover, since patients have a long-term relationship with their physicians and the two parties come to know each other well, physicians are adept at determining the genuine desires of their patients in medical treatment situations in which the patients might not be able to communicate their wishes. In addition, they are able to diagnose depression as opposed to a true wish to go through the euthanasia process. As a testament to the enduring nature of the relationship between physician and patient, almost half of all of the individuals who die in the Netherlands die at home under the care of their general practitioner.[3] Patients may decide, however, that they can best be cared for at a medical facility rather than at home. An important difference in the Dutch medical system lies in the development of advanced pain management and treatment in a hospicelike setting. Palliative pain care is extremely progressive, and care centers are located adjacent to nearly every hospital.

The unique situation that exists with euthanasia and physician-assisted suicide practices in the Netherlands is due to an unusual combination of historical factors in the development of the trusting physician-patient relationship and the extraordinary level of health care services available to all citizens. Economics does not influence medical decisions at the end of life, as the medical institutional system does not stand to profit from these choices and the family of the patient is not burdened with health care expenses. Working in conjunction with these factors is the fundamental nature of the governmental system itself. Because the powers of the ruling monarch are constrained by the constitution, the populace has a greater impact on the decision-making process with respect to social concerns. Industrialization serves to increase education standards for the country as a whole and naturally raises literacy levels, creating a more intelligent, vocal, effective, socially aware, and politically active citizenry.

In the Netherlands, euthanasia and physician-assisted suicide are regularly and openly practiced; however, technically they are not allowed by statute. The national *Penal Code* clearly specifies this position in Articles 293 and 294. These articles were enacted in the late nineteenth century to distinguish euthanasia from murder and to designate different punishments. Article 293 defines euthanasia as a criminal offense. It states, "He, who, on the explicit and serious desire of another person, deprives him of his life, will be punished by imprisonment up to 12 years or a fine in the 5th category." Article 294 defines assistance in committing suicide as a criminal offense and reads, "He, who deliberately incites another person to commit suicide, renders assistance in doing so or provides him with the means to do so, will, in case suicide follows, be punished with an imprisonment up to three years or a fine in the 4th category." Instead of directly legalizing euthanasia and assisted suicide, a gradual series of judicial steps, which has been implemented since 1973, has allowed physicians conforming to certain guidelines to go unpunished. The legal system permits physicians to present a standard defense if they have stringently adhered to this set of strict rules in euthanasia or physician-assisted suicide procedures.[4]

World War II Nazi "euthanasia" activities still have a strong impact on the moral aspects of the euthanasia debate in the Netherlands.[5] Throughout the World War II German occupation of the Netherlands, many physicians chose to go to concentration camps rather than reveal the names of their patients, who would ultimately become candidates for the Nazi's euthanasia program. This well-known historical fact is one of the primary reasons that a relationship of deep trust is felt between physicians and patients. In 1941, Arthur Seyss-Inquart issued what appeared at first to be an innocent directive. Physicians quickly translated the "Order of the Reich Commissar for the Occupied Territories Concerning the Netherlands Doctors" to mean that they were to help carry out Germany's "euthanasia" program. They refused to follow the order, and many began practicing medicine in a clandestine manner so as not to be persecuted and punished for their unwillingness to comply with Seyss-Inquart's request. Their adamant refusal to follow the directive led Seyss-Inquart to arrest more than a hundred physicians and deport them to concentration camps. The remaining physicians nobly held their ground and, subsequently, never allowed involuntary euthanasia to be practiced in the Netherlands.[6] Seyss-Inquart was later executed for his war crimes.

In the 1960s, the medical profession more than any other group brought the discussion of euthanasia to the forefront in the Netherlands. The ethical and moral issue of patients enduring extended, agonizing, and painful deaths as a result of improved medical technology began to be publicly discussed, and physicians began to openly disobey the tenets of Articles 293 and 294. When these physicians were convicted of killing a patient, they generally received either no sentence or an insubstantial one. In 1973, a mercy-killing case that came before the court gave rise to the eventual acceptance of voluntary euthanasia for the terminally ill. Two years prior, Dr. Geertruida Postma administered a fatal injection of morphine to her terminally ill mother, who was committed to a nursing home and had begged to die. Her mother had suffered a cerebral hemorrhage, was partially paralyzed and deaf, experienced difficulty in speaking, and at the time had pneumonia. On one visit to the nursing home, Dr. Postma found her mother tied to the arms of a chair and described her as "a human wreck, hanging in that chair."[7] Dr. Postma returned the next day and injected her mother with the fatal dose of morphine. She relayed her actions to the director of the facility, and he telephoned the police and reported the incident.

Dr. Postma was charged with mercy killing, which carried a penalty of up to twelve years in prison. During the trial, Postma received strong support from the public. The Society for Voluntary Euthanasia was formed during this period and would eventually go on to become the largest of its kind in the world. In addition, the Foundation for Voluntary Euthanasia was developed by a group of academics to explore the questions of euthanasia in detail. Dr. Postma was ultimately found guilty by the court, but the judge imposed only a one-week suspended sentence, stating that it was proper to administer pain-relieving drugs to the patient if the goal was the relief of physical pain, even if death resulted from the medication. In this case, however, Dr. Postma's intention was the death of her mother, not simply pain relief. The string of court decisions that followed set the precedent for the defense of force majeure (superior force) for physicians who performed euthanasia on terminally ill patients. It was recognized that the physician was in a position of a conflict of duties between that of following the law and that of honoring the needs of the patient. The law simply became unenforceable.

The Rotterdam Court, the Royal Dutch Medical Association, and the Remmelink Report

In 1981, the Rotterdam criminal court established guidelines for noncriminal aid in dying, and over time these guidelines have been broadly interpreted. They include that the patient must "be suffering from unbearable pain; the patient must be conscious; the desire to die must be enduring; the decision to die must be given freely and voluntarily; the patient must have been given alternatives to euthanasia and time to consider the alternatives; no reasonable solution to the problem must exist; the death of the patient cannot inflict unnecessary suffering on others; more than one person must be involved in the euthanasia decision; the patient must have a clear understanding of his condition; and extreme care must be taken in actually making the final euthanasia decision."[8] It is important to note that nowhere does it state that the patient must be terminally ill or that the suffering must be of a physical nature.

In 1984, the Royal Dutch Medical Association made a dramatic departure from all other medical associations in the world by proposing similar guidelines to those of the Rotterdam court. They proposed "rules of carefulness" under which medically administered euthanasia could be justified, rules that were greatly abbreviated compared to those of the Rotterdam court. They proposed that euthanasia not be prosecuted in court (1) if the mentally competent patient made freely and knowingly and repeatedly documented requests for euthanasia, (2) if the patient experienced untreatable, unrelievable pain (the illness did not have to be terminal), and (3) if the physician in charge of the patient consulted at least one other physician, who agreed that euthanasia was the only solution. Further the physician was not obligated to perform euthanasia but could instead refer the patient to another physician.[9] Before the Royal Dutch Medical Association proposed its rules, euthanasia was practiced with little attention from either the government or the medical community. During this time period, most of the deaths that resulted from euthanasia went unreported, probably to protect the physician from possible prosecution and to protect the privacy of the grieving family. Studies indicate that if euthanasia and assisted-suicide data had been reported, they would have stimulated an open discussion about the topic and brought the issue to the forefront.[10]

In 1990, in an effort to improve official notification of deaths precipitated by euthanasia, procedural changes were implemented. These changes include having the physician inform the medical examiner (or coroner) of the circumstances of the death instead of declaring a natural death. The medical examiner then reports to the district attorney (or chief prosecutor), who reviews the procedure and concludes whether an investigation should be initiated.[11] The Royal Dutch Medical Association and the Ministry of Justice agreed on the notification procedure, which was eventually incorporated into the 1994 Burial Act.[12] Later that year, the government commissioned the first scientific examination of euthanasia practices in the Netherlands. J. Remmelink, attorney general of the Dutch Supreme Court, spearheaded the study.

The Remmelink study investigated the practice of euthanasia and other "medical decisions concerning the end of life" (also phrased as "medical decisions at the end of life"), or MDEL. Euthanasia was operationalized to mean "a life-ending act by someone other than the patient and at his or her request."[13] Physicians who participated in the research were granted immunity from prosecution for information that they contributed. The three types of MDEL are administering pain medications in dosages that could shorten the patient's life (alleviating pain and suffering); withholding treatment where in all likelihood it would have extended the life of the patient (nontreatment); and providing or administering drugs to the patient with the express intent to hasten death (euthanasia, assisted suicide, and death without explicit and repeated requests). The investigators examined the circumstances of 130,000 deaths in the Netherlands in 1990.

On September 10, 1991, the results of the *Remmelink Report* were released. The report found that there were approximately 9,000 requests for either euthanasia or assisted suicide per year. Of these 9,000 individuals who requested the procedure, only about one-third actually received it. The study predicted that 38 percent of all deaths were as a result of one of the three categories of MDEL. In the category of voluntary euthanasia, the study estimated that 1.8 percent, or approximately 2,300 individuals, died in this manner. Assisted suicide accounted for 0.3 percent of deaths, and 35 percent of deaths resulted from turning off respirators, withholding treatment, or providing morphine to alleviate pain and suffering. The most controversial finding was that in approximately 1,000 deaths, or 0.8 percent of the cases, physicians took measures to deliberately end patients' lives without their express consent, repeated requests, or knowledge. In the majority of these instances, the patient had previously expressed a wish for voluntary euthanasia, was suffering excessive, observable pain from cancer, and death was accelerated by mere hours or a few days.[14] Those requesting euthanasia most often suffered from cancer and ranged in age from thirty-five to seventy years. The most frequently cited reasons for asking to die were "unbearable suffering" and "hopeless situation." Only 486 physician-assisted deaths had been reported on all death certificates issued in the Netherlands. It is difficult to determine if the situation had improved or deteriorated from previous years, as no data prior to this study exist.

Public Opinion Data

Two surveys have been conducted as a follow-up to the *Remmelink Report*. One study compared euthanasia and assisted-suicide practices in 1995 with those in 1990 to determine if the Netherlands had launched on a slippery slope. The other study evaluated the effects of the new notification procedure guidelines.

The first study found that the practice of euthanasia increased only slightly, from causing 1.8 percent of all deaths in 1990 to 2.4 percent in 1995. The authors hypothesized that the increase could be attributed to the aging of the population and the increased mortality from cancer (the most common disease in cases of euthanasia). Instances of assisted suicide appeared to remain relatively rare, probably due to the fact that lethal drugs taken orally may take up to three hours to be effective before death comes to the patient (thus, a seemingly more humane option than mere minutes from a lethal injection), and while no significant moral distinction is drawn between the two acts by the Dutch, assisted suicide is less desirable.

Two other issues of interest come to light from the study. First, only 5 percent of the requests for assistance in dying came from patients who said they were experiencing unbearable pain. Thus, pain itself does not appear to be the most significant factor in the patient's decision to pursue euthanasia. Second, the fear that the elderly are being coerced by loved ones into choosing euthanasia is simply not true. Euthanasia in patients over the age of eighty is rare. Patients between the ages of fifty-five and seventy-five suffering from cancer request euthanasia or physician-assisted suicide most frequently. In addition, the number of physicians who stated that they ended a patient's life without explicit consent or request dropped from 27 percent to 23 percent. The authors concluded that there is no danger of the system being abused.

With respect to notification procedures, the second study showed that physician-assisted suicide reporting increased significantly, from 18 percent in 1990 to 41 percent in 1995. Still, almost 60 percent of the cases remained unreported. Many physicians believed the new reporting procedures to be burdensome, especially considering the multiple levels of legal review. While physicians believed the guidelines to be necessary, they were discouraged by the fact that euthanasia and assisted suicide technically remained illegal even though official guidelines existed. Many physicians simply did not want to risk the chance of prosecution under these conditions.[15]

Current Legal Status

One case in particular tested the boundaries of the existing euthanasia guidelines. In 1991, Dr. Chabot, a psychiatrist, helped a physically healthy woman, who was neither terminally ill nor mentally handicapped, to commit suicide. The woman was experiencing intolerable mental suffering as a result of a divorce from her husband after an extremely violent marriage, followed by the deaths of her only two children from cancer. She first sought assistance from the Dutch Federation for Voluntary Euthanasia, which referred her to Dr. Chabot. It became apparent to him that she was severely depressed and genuinely desired to die. Dr. Chabot consulted with several other professional colleagues about the case, but none of these colleagues actually performed an examination on his patient. He agreed to help her terminate her life and gave her a fatal dose of drugs. Dr. Chabot was charged with her death under Article 294 of the *Dutch Penal Code*. The lower court found the psychiatrist not guilty on the grounds that the euthanasia guidelines could be interpreted broadly. The Supreme Court overturned this verdict and found the psychiatrist guilty, although he was not prosecuted. They held that in situations in which the individual requested euthanasia on the basis of "unbearable psychic suffering," a minimum of two physicians must examine the individual before any action can be taken.[16] Another study revealed that psychiatrists seldom comply with these requests. It was estimated that between two and five assisted deaths occur each year in this type of case and that most of these individuals were at the end of a terminal illness.[17]

The case is important because the court held for the first time in history that psychological suffering could fall within the definition of unbearable suffering. The court further recognized that it is almost impossible to determine whether the patient's request for euthanasia or assisted suicide was voluntary and thoughtful or stemmed from the effects of the mental illness or incapacity. As a result of this case, the Dutch government announced that the guidelines would be altered to include the stipulation that the physician must consult two independent specialists when euthanasia or assisted suicide is requested and that at least one of the specialists be a psychiatrist.

In 1993, the Dutch Parliament agreed to endorse euthanasia under certain conditions. Still, no legal right to euthanasia existed, and physicians could be prosecuted if the guidelines were not followed. Among the guidelines are that the patient's request for euthanasia or assisted suicide must be durable, the patient must be suffering from unbearable pain without the chance of relief, the decision must be made under noncoercive conditions, and the patient must have a clear understanding of his or her condition.[18] In 1995, the Royal Dutch Medical Association's guidelines were revised. The first change was that assisted suicide is preferable to euthanasia. Next, consulting physicians who provide their opinions should not be connected to either the patient or the physician. Lastly, if the attending physician is opposed to euthanasia and assisted suicide, he or she has the obligation to locate another physician who is willing to perform euthanasia or assisted suicide.

In a newsletter originating from the International Conference of the World Federation of Right-to-Die Societies in Melbourne, Australia, in October 1996, Derek Humphry, a distinguished proponent of the right-to-die movement, stated that he believed there would be new legislation in the Netherlands in the coming years that would enshrine the current guidelines and make euthanasia technically legal.[19] This would serve to remove much of the stigma attached to the act.

The United Kingdom of Great Britain and Northern Ireland

The euthanasia movement commenced quite early in the United Kingdom, with the British Voluntary Euthanasia Society being formed in

1935 by Lord Moynihan and Dr. Killick Millard. The following year, King George V died prematurely through euthanasia with the assistance of his physician, Lord Dawson, who consulted with Queen Mary and discovered that it was her desire not to let the king's pain and discomfort continue. Later that same year, the Voluntary Euthanasia Bill, which sought to legalize euthanasia under certain restrictive conditions for suffering, terminally ill patients and others who wanted it, was introduced into the House of Lords. It was easily defeated. The next euthanasia bill was not introduced into the House of Lords until 1969. The bill was long-titled: "An Act to provide in certain circumstances for the administration of euthanasia to persons who request it and who are suffering from an irremediable condition, and to enable persons to request in advance the administration of euthanasia in the event of their suffering from such a condition at a future date." This bill was broader in scope and far less restrictive than the 1936 bill; it too was defeated.

The Incurable Patients Bill of 1976 attempted to clearly identify rights already universally agreed upon at the common law level. Such rights included the ability to refuse unwanted life-sustaining medical treatment, the allowance of sufficient quantities of drugs to relieve pain or distress, and the right to be rendered unconscious should no means of relief exist. There was no denying that these rights already existed, but opponents of the bill feared that explicitly stating these principles in written form would lead patients to interpret it to mean that euthanasia would be a readily available, legal medical option. In an effort to provide information and assistance to patients who wished to end their lives, the British Voluntary Euthanasia Society produced a self-help book on suicide in response to the relative inaction of the medical community. The society agreed that the publication, temporarily titled *A Guide to Self-Deliverance*, would be offered only to members over twenty-five years of age. The idea was met with tremendous controversy, as the Suicide Act of 1961 called for imprisonment for a period of up to fourteen years for anyone who assisted suicide, and it still was questionable as to whether disseminating information about how to successfully complete the act was technically assisting suicide. In 1980, the Voluntary Euthanasia Society of Scotland separated from the British Voluntary Euthanasia Society in order to publish the world's first self-deliverance book, *How to Die with Dignity*.

In spite of early efforts by the euthanasia societies, both euthanasia and physician-assisted suicide remain illegal in the United Kingdom. Suicide has been legal in Scotland since time immemorial, but in England only since 1961. Although suicide was legalized, assistance with suicide was not. The Suicide Act of 1961 specifically states in S2(1) that "a person who aids, abets, counsels or procures the suicide of another, or an attempt by another to commit suicide, shall be liable on conviction on indictment to imprisonment for a term not exceeding fourteen years." As there is no defined criminal offense for assisting or abetting suicide in Scotland, and as it has never been illegal, the Suicide Act of 1961 probably does not apply there, but this has yet to be fully tested by law or determined by the court.[20] Although neither euthanasia nor physician-assisted suicide is legal, the patient who is mentally competent does maintain the right to refuse medical treatment and life-sustaining nourishment. Subjecting the patient to unwanted medical treatment would be considered an assault under both criminal and civil law.[21]

In 1995, *Advance Statements about Medical Treatment* was issued by the British Medical Association at the request of the House of Lords Committee on Medical Ethics. The report detailed advance statements that patients can make concerning what future medical treatment they desire to receive should mental incapacity develop as a result of illness, accident, or other peril. The code declared that these advance statements may contain the name of an individual (other than the patient) who has decision-making capacity for the patient, shares the patient's beliefs and values, and knows the patient's preferences in terms of medical treatment. Physicians are not legally bound to follow all advance statements but are expected to respect patients' wishes if possible. In addition, two other types of statement have legal impetus in the United Kingdom, one in which patients specify that they want no life-sustaining treatment after irreversible deterioration (permanent vegetative state) and one in which patients specify that they do not want any medical procedures performed.[22] The code does not address euthanasia or physician-assisted suicide specifically.

Influential Case Histories

A few cases have brought to light the struggle the United Kingdom faces in trying to balance the needs of the terminally ill and those of the state and society. One of the first trials to test these waters was that of Dr. Bodkin Adams in 1957. Dr. Adams stood accused of murdering one of his elderly patients. He maintained throughout the trial that he only attempted to alleviate the pain and suffering of his patient. Dr. Adams was well respected within his community and well regarded by his patients. It was, however, not unusual during this era for patients to remember their personal physician in their wills. The suspicion, of course, was that Dr. Adams accelerated the death of his patient in order to receive a bequest. Dr. Adams held that the fees he would have collected had his patient remained alive for a longer period of time would have greatly outweighed any gift that might have been left to him through his patient's will. Fortunately for Dr. Adams, the prosecutor was not successful in proving that he had delivered the fatal dose to his patient, and he was subsequently found guilty of only minor charges related to misuse of drugs.[23] The case was one of the first to examine the principle of the double effect—one act having two consequences: in the case of euthanasia, this would imply administering increased doses of analgesics to alleviate pain that may have the added effect of hastening death.

In 1992, Dr. Nigel Cox was found guilty of the attempted murder of his long-time patient Lillian Boyes. Boyes experienced unrelievable agonies from her condition, including ulcers and abscesses on all of her appendages and fractured vertebrae. The pain was so severe that she would "howl like a dog" whenever she was touched. In her final days, she repeatedly requested assistance in dying from Dr. Cox. He ultimately succumbed to her wish and administered a lethal dose of potassium chloride. Dr. Cox recorded the death as caused by bronchopneumonia. A nurse who read Boyes's chart became suspicious and reported Dr. Cox to the authorities. Dr. Cox was suspended from his position, and a charge of attempted murder was filed (as Boyes's body had been cremated and no evidence remained). During the trial, the defense maintained that Dr. Cox's motive was to ease Boyes's pain, not to kill her. The jury found Dr. Cox guilty of attempted murder, but the judge suspended the sentence. Dr. Cox received immense support from the public for his apparent merciful action and was eventually offered his position back, subject to his acceptance of stipulations, including learning more about pain control. The trial heightened awareness of the issue and generated intense public interest, debate, and publicity both for and against the practice of euthanasia.[24]

In 1993, the issue of living wills came to the forefront in the United Kingdom with the case of a young teenager, Anthony Bland. Bland had remained in a persistent vegetative state for three years before the court allowed the cessation of parenteral nutrition.[25] The judges presiding over the case were in agreement that Bland's tube feeding should be considered nonbeneficial treatment and that the primary physician was under no duty to continue providing it. The judges stated that had Bland let his future health care treatment wishes be known through a living will, he would have been permitted to die earlier. Lord Justice Hoffman attempted to bridge the differences among the legal considerations, the medical issues, and moral reasoning: "In my view, the choice which the law makes must reassure people that the courts do have full respect for life, but that they do not pursue the principle to the point at which it has become almost empty of any real content and when it involves the sacrifice of other important values such as human dignity and freedom of choice."[26] The importance of advance directives was pivotal in this case.

In Northern Ireland, the Supreme Court ruled in 1995 that life support could be withdrawn from a woman who had been in a near-persistent vegetative state for twenty-three years. The woman's family had previously gained the right to withdraw her feeding tube, but the institution she was in and the attorney general of Northern Ireland jointly appealed the decision. The life support that was removed involved a gastrostomy feeding tube, which the court held to be "intrusive" and interfered with the integrity of her body. The Catholic Church, members of the medical profession, and other pro-life groups expressed great concern with this ruling. The Fellowship of Catholic Schools stated that this decision "outstripped the Nazis and provided the State with a constitutionally correct alibi for euthanasia in Ireland."[27] This was the first time a ruling on this matter had been issued in Northern Ireland.

In England that same year, a boy under the age of two, who was born severely brain damaged, deaf, and subject to seizures when touched and who had to be constantly sedated due to extreme pain, was made a ward of the court in order to have life-sustaining treatment withdrawn. Hospital physicians would not remove the life-sustaining feeding tube without a court order mandating them to do so. While abortion is legal in the country if the child will be severely handicapped, no law exists to prematurely terminate the life of a hopelessly ill or handicapped child.[28] Euthanasia and physician-assisted suicide remain unlawful, and it is a criminal offense to aid, abet, assist, and counsel in suicide.

A Scottish court in 1996 decided that Paul Brady would not receive any jail time for putting an end to his brother James's suffering by giving him alcohol, pills, and finally suffocating him with a pillow. Before his death, James was battling a slow, agonizing death from Huntington's chorea and was released from a nursing home so he could spend the Christmas holidays with his family. The judge stated that he believed Paul acted out of compassion for his brother and that Paul only complied with James's wishes after he had made repeated, heartfelt requests for assistance in dying.[29] The judge further emphasized that no jail term was imposed due to the exceptional circumstances of the case. The brothers had witnessed their mother die from the same disease, and Paul could not tolerate James suffering the same fate.

A highly publicized and tragic mercy murder was that of Jeremy Debonnaire. Debonnaire, who suffered from lung cancer and experienced pain that he believed he could no longer tolerate, feared that his family would not collect insurance policy benefits if he committed suicide, so he checked himself out of the hospital in October 1996 and hired two hit men to kill him by shooting him in the head to make it look as if a robbery had occurred. A close friend of Debonnaire's had been instructed to pay the assassins after his death. Two men were arrested for the crime but were later released for lack of evidence. Debonnaire's family has called for the perpetrators to be brought to justice, reasoning that pain itself does not make a life worthless.[30]

In June 1997, David Hainsworth received a two-year probation sentence in Scotland for attempting to kill his cancer-stricken, eighty-two year-old father. Hainsworth pled guilty to the lesser charge of assaulting his father, after unsuccessfully attempting to smother him with a pillow. Relatives prevailed in preventing Hainsworth from killing his father at the time, but the father died a few days later, while his son was in jail. Hainsworth had moved back to the area to care for his father and watched him grow progressively ill. After the incident, relatives wrote letters of forgiveness, which were presented to the court in hopes of a lenient sentence. The distress, strain, and intense emotional pressures of caring for the terminally ill, combined with the lack of legal, medical, and social recourses, were demonstrated by this case.

In July 1997, two physicians, Dr. Michael Irwin and Dr. David Moor, accelerated the euthanasia debate in the United Kingdom by publicly announcing that they had committed euthanasia many times during their long careers. The two went public with the announcement to "highlight the hypocrisy surrounding euthanasia" and demonstrate the extreme risk physicians take in performing either euthanasia or physician-assisted suicide. They face possible life imprisonment (through the charge of murder) stemming from the euthanasia charge (voluntary mercy killing) or up to fourteen years in prison for assisting the patient with suicide. Dr. Irwin, who is chairman of the British Voluntary Euthanasia Society, points to the common use of the double-effect treatment and to physicians who sanctimoniously act surprised that the patient would die after large, successive doses of painkillers. Dr. Irwin believes that the double effect is, in reality, a slow way to commit euthanasia and is already frequently used in hospices. Dr. Irwin and Dr. Moor aim to create an atmosphere in which euthanasia is a viable option for patients and in which physicians can be honest about their course of treatment. They believe an interim step to the legalization of euthanasia would be an amendment to the Suicide Act of 1961 permitting physician assistance to terminally ill patients wishing to commit suicide.[31] On July 31, 1997, Dr. Moor was arrested and charged with the death of his patient, George Liddell, who was eighty-five and suffering from cancer. Dr. Moor has insisted that he only provided pain relief to Liddell in his final stages of cancer.

Public Opinion Data

As in many other countries, in the United Kingdom there appears to be an increasing struggle between the law, which forbids euthanasia, and public opinion, which shows growing support for euthanasia.[32] In 1993, a national opinion poll demonstrated that 79 percent of respondents agreed with the statement, The law should allow adults to receive medical help to a peaceful death if suffering from an incurable illness that is intolerable to them, provided that they have previously requested such help in writing.[33] The British Social Attitudes Survey is an impartial examination of the country's changing social values. The data are gathered through an annual national survey and are produced by Social and Community Planning Research, Great Britain's largest research facility. In the 1996–97 edition of the survey, 82 percent of individuals polled favored a law permitting physicians to end the lives of patients with "a painful incurable disease." A decade prior, the figure was 75 percent in support of euthanasia.

At the other end of the spectrum, the survey found that a mere 12 percent believed that euthanasia should be available to those who are "simply tired of living and wish to die," and 51 percent supported the option of euthanasia for individuals who are not in a great deal of pain but who have become totally dependent on relatives for all of their needs. Only 2 percent of those polled had made a living will, but three out of four said that physicians should be allowed to honor the patient's end-of-life wishes if they have been previously documented in a living will.[34] Another report, published in 1996, found that 80 percent agreed with the statement, Human beings should have the right to choose when to die. Of these, 42 percent preferred voluntary euthanasia as the method of attaining death with dignity, while 28 percent chose physician-assisted suicide; 22 percent had no opinion on a preferred method of dying. In a separate survey of practitioners and pharmacists, the same report found that 54 percent supported a change in the existing law to allow physician-assisted suicide under certain circumstances. The survey also revealed that medical practitioners preferred physician-assisted suicide to voluntary euthanasia by a margin of 43 percent to 19 percent.[35]

A 1997 survey of 1,032 physicians in Northern Ireland revealed that slightly more than 20 percent of Northern Irish physicians support physician-assisted suicide; 14 percent of these physicians reported being asked to assist in hastening death for terminally ill patients. When asked if they would comply with a request of this nature, 13 percent said they would. Physicians are permitted to withhold extraordinary treatment to sustain a patient if they judge it to be medically appropriate. In addition, they must observe a patient's request to withhold treatment. When administering medication, however, the intent of the physician must be solely to relieve pain, not to cause death. The Medical Council of Northern Ireland is currently reviewing its code of ethics for Northern Irish physicians. It is not expected that there will be any alterations to the euthanasia or physician-assisted suicide policy in the foreseeable future.[36]

Germany

As a result of Hitler's "euthanasia program," Germany approaches the issue from a unique vantage point. Article 1 of the Constitution of the Federal Republic of Germany states that "the dignity of a person is inviolable. All state authorities are obliged to respect and protect it." While the act of suicide has been legal since 1751, under this constitutionally imposed directive, euthanasia remains illegal. Physician-assisted suicide is practiced, but certain guidelines must be rigidly adhered to when assisting with a suicide to avoid possible prosecution.[37] First, individuals who wish to die must be able to exercise control over their actions and, second, must be acting of their own free will.[38] Thus, assisting the suicide efforts of a mentally incompetent individual or the coercing of an individual into the act would be strictly forbidden.

With regard to life-prolonging measures, before 1994, German physicians were legally permitted only to cease life-sustaining treatment for dying patients. Germany's constitutional court ruled in 1994 that physicians could now apply this procedure to terminally ill patients as well.[39] Germany, however, faces a unique situation with the euthanasia question. Because in the not-so-distant past, the Nazi regime referred to its initiative to purify the German race as "euthanasia," the word takes on a significantly different connotation and stigma.

On July 25, 1933, Hitler instituted the Law for the Prevention of Progeny with Hereditary Diseases, with the purpose of eliminating those with supposed hereditary diseases from the German "race." In six years, it is estimated that 375,000 Germans were involuntarily sterilized.[40] In addition to sterilization, this law legalized abortion for women who were going through the sterilization procedure. The law was broadened to include Gypsies, Jews, and Poles, in an attempt to decrease ethnic minorities in Germany. Hitler's "euthanasia" program, initiated in 1938 and 1939, was aimed at ridding Germany of what he considered defective and unworthy individuals, including the mentally ill, the handicapped, those suffering from incurable illnesses, the aged, and imperfect newborns.[41] The stated motivations for this program were eugenics (purifying the "Aryan" race) and economics.[42] Hitler wanted to avoid the financial burden on public health care for these individuals.[43] In addition, Hitler considered keeping these "useless individuals" alive a waste of food supplies during Germany's wartime efforts.[44] He next moved to eliminate so-called defective races of people, including Jews, Gypsies, Russians, and Poles.[45]

Memories of the Nazi euthanasia program linger in the minds of many Germans today, but perhaps time will dim these memories so that euthanasia can be openly discussed and debated in German society without the stigma.

Contemporary Germans make a clear distinction between euthanasia and physician-assisted suicide. Many Germans still associate involuntary euthanasia with the Nazi atrocities rather than the overstepping of medical boundaries by physicians and other health care providers who take matters into their own hands (although this did happen during Hitler's reign). There is the added complication that, while assisted suicide is not illegal, German law stipulates situations in which an obligation is imposed on certain professionals and other individuals to rescue an individual from a suicide attempt. Thus, physicians are faced with a legal paradox: While they may legally provide lethal drugs to hasten death, physicians assume a duty to resuscitate patients once they have taken the drug and become unconscious. Currently, this legal contradiction, which effectively forces individuals to seek assistance outside the medical community, is under scrutiny. Speculation regarding the existing law to provide rescue assistance for suicide victims holds that this obligation could possibly extend to spouses and close friends.

Germany has an advanced health care system composed of two primary divisions, office based and hospital based. Office-based physicians (about 40 percent of Germany's physicians) typically do not provide treatment for patients in hospitals, and hospital-based physicians rarely have appointments outside of the hospital. Individuals have free access to primary-care physicians in the office-based facilities. The German health care system is not operated by the government directly; instead, statutory health insurance funds, also called sickness funds, are administered through self-governing insurance companies that effectively cover 90 percent of the population. The government, however, regulates the levels of benefits received, determines national policy, and provides guidance in fiscal operations. The services rendered include unlimited hospital care, maternity care, prescription drugs, and dental visits. The insurance funds also provide for unemployed and retired individuals."[46]

When death is imminent or when the patient is incompetent, consent will often be sought from the family. In Germany, living wills are seldom used, and the durable power of attorney has been legally permissible only since 1992. Do-not-resuscitate orders are infrequently documented, and it is considered a matter that is generally discussed with the family, not the patient. Patients' advance directives are given consideration by physicians when the patient is competent, patients' wishes are explicitly expressed, and patients have family support. In most instances, however, the physician continues to render decisions concerning life-sustaining treatment for the patient with the acquiescence of the family. When the physician and the patient's family differ in their view of the appropriate course of treatment, the physician's opinion will, in most cases, prevail.[47]

Because of the incongruities within the German legal system and medical community, several groups have been active in the debate on euthanasia. Since 1980 the Deutsche Gesellschaft fur humanness Sterben (DGHS), or the German Society for Humane Dying, has advocated using suicide and assisted suicide to achieve a dignified, painless death. The society is primarily concerned with providing accurate information to individuals who are considering suicide and with assisting patients in making end-of-life treatment decisions. The society also works to verify the information it supplies to individuals by conducting extensive research on its members who have either committed suicide (information provided by the assistant to the suicide victim) or attempted suicide. The collection of information is facilitated by the fact that assisted suicide is not illegal and there is no fear of legal repercussions or other ramifications to the information provider. The society has also prepared legislation, including a bill that would effectively repeal Paragraph 216 of the *German Criminal Code*, which calls for punishment for "killing on request." Other legislation calls for the conformation of the contemporary individual legal provisions to that of German constitutional standards, human rights, and the European Convention for the Protection of Human Rights and Fundamental Freedoms.

Switzerland

Like its neighboring countries of France and Germany, Switzerland has not legalized euthanasia. But there is no sanction against either physician-assisted suicide or assisted suicide. In fact, Switzerland has permitted both since 1937. As euthanasia is not represented within the Swiss Code of Law, the Swiss Academy of Medical Sciences has taken it upon itself to develop a set of directives on euthanasia. While these directives do not have legal validity, they are nonetheless widely observed. Assisted suicide has been governed by Articles 114 and 115 of the *Swiss*

Penal Code, which state that it is not a criminal offense if there is no personal motive for or gain through the assistance. The reason for assisting the individual must be "pure and noble" in nature. Article 63 of the *Swiss Penal Code* further states that a judge may "mete out punishment in accordance with the guilt of the actor; he shall consider the motives, the prior life, and the personal circumstances of the guilty person."[48] In addition, the judge may take into consideration the particular circumstances of the patient. For example the judge may mitigate the sentence after determining if the individual had a terminal illness, experienced intractable pain and suffering, or made persistent, repeated requests for death. Of the 100–120 reported instances of deaths from assisted suicide each year, a mere 20 cite the involvement of physicians.[49] A case of alleged abuse of an assisted suicide act has yet to be brought before the courts in Switzerland.

The influential Swiss right-to-die organization, EXIT Suisse Romande, approached the Geneva government in May 1993 with a petition requesting an added article in the health bill to legally recognize a patient's living will or death-with-dignity wish. EXIT based its argument on the premise that patients have fundamental democratic rights to have their medical directives followed. The petition was adopted by the High Council of the Canton of Geneva in March 1996. EXIT also submitted questions to the Swiss Parliament attempting to discern the federal government's position on formally legalizing medical assistance for euthanasia under specific conditions.[50]

The health care system in Switzerland is privatized. The advanced technological state of the health care system is reflected in the high average life expectancy of seventy-nine years of age. As in any industrialized society, living and working conditions are such that infectious diseases no longer cause the majority of deaths. Cancer, heart disease, AIDS, and other terminal illnesses require treatment with state-of-the-art medical technology that are expensive to administer and that artificially extend life beyond its natural length. In any country in which such advanced care is possible and in which health care is private, there are economic incentives for the patient's family to pursue euthanasia or physician-assisted suicide. The privatized medical community has a financial incentive to keep the patient alive as long as possible, because a live patient (especially one that requires extensive treatment) generates revenue, whereas an empty bed does not.

Spain

Although euthanasia and physician-assisted suicide are not legal medical treatment options in Spain, this does not mean that Spain has been unresponsive to right-to-die concerns. One of the most famous right-to-die cases in Spain is that of Ramon Sanpedro. Sanpedro was completely paralyzed in a swimming accident in his youth and has fought for his right to die since 1993. With the assistance of the Spanish right-to-die society, Derecho a Morir Dignamente, Sanpedro has brought his case to the highest court, the Constitutional Court of Spain. Sanpedro, who has been seeking the right to die through assisted suicide, published a book, *Letters from Hell*, in which he discusses his efforts to free himself of his extreme pain and suffering. He has characterized himself and his current debilitating condition as "a head attached to a corpse." The courts have thus far held that it is the duty of the legislature, not the court, to alter the penal code regarding active euthanasia. The justices further stated that euthanasia is acceptable in a moral sense as well as from a scientific and social standpoint.[51]

Derecho a Morir Dignamente's primary goals are to obtain legal recognition for the right to die with dignity, to defend the right of terminally ill patients to die peacefully without suffering, and to promote the right of all individuals to select the time and means to end their lives. The group also advocates the abolition of the century-old punishment for euthanasia. There is a movement under way to reduce the penalty to a three-year prison sentence. A member of the voluntary euthanasia society, Juanxo Dominguez, who is also a member of parliament, presented a proposal to the Basque government for a law on advance directives. Even though the proposal was rejected, many associates were pleased with the fact that the initiative was introduced.[52]

With the death of General Francisco Franco in 1975 and the formation of a democratic government in Spain, the Ministry of Health was restored and the National Institute of Public Health Care was created. The National Institute of Public Health Care undertook the managerial functions of public health care. It operates in conjunction with both the Ministry of Health, which provides direction for health care organization and policy development, and the Ministry of Labor and Social Security, which oversees administrative aspects such as budgeting. Under this policy, 99 percent of the Spanish population has the right to free health care coverage.[53] Approximately 90 percent of all Spanish hospitals are publicly administered; 10 percent are privately owned. Privately owned hospitals cost the patient two or three times that of a public hospital.[54]

As is typical in many countries, in Spain the quality of health care treatment improves in or near urban areas, and the provisions for health care are somewhat uneven throughout the rest of the country. Spain has the traditional social welfare benefits, including retirement benefits and unemployment insurance, along with a national health care system. But benefits from the welfare system tend to be less comprehensive than in other Western European countries. The rapid industrialization of Spain is reflected in falling birth rates and increased life expectancy. The average life expectancy of a Spaniard is a high seventy-seven years. This, in turn, has created a rapidly aging population, which will require even more welfare services from the government. With this increasing aged population and the resulting increases in health care and retirement costs, Spain may be more willing to examine its stance on euthanasia and physician-assisted suicide as legitimate medical options.

France

Euthanasia and physician-assisted suicide are prohibited in France. These procedures are forbidden to such an extent that even literature about them can be difficult to obtain. In 1986, when the controversial book *Final Exit* by Derek Humphry was released in France, the government imposed a censorship law and dispatched police to seize copies. The book details methods of how the terminally ill can take matters into their own hands and end their own suffering without the assistance of a physician. The book is specifically directed toward the terminally ill; unfortunately, however, the contents can be used by those who are not terminally ill but who are seeking to die for other reasons. Humphry's publisher retrieved the books before the police could get to them and shipped them to Belgium. *Final Exit* remains banned in France.

The Federation Mondiale des Societes pour le Droit de Mourir dans la Dignite, a right-to-die society, is the most active group of its type in France. The society believes that several legitimate arguments support death-with-dignity concerns in industrialized countries. Like many other industrialized countries, France has the medical technology to prolong life in cases of chronic and terminal illnesses. The society holds that the negative aspects of advanced medical technology should be fully examined; medical technology serves to extend the time patients live even when their lives are unbearable. Many of these suffering patients, the society maintains, simply wish to die a natural death in a natural time frame. They advocate the right of patients to request medication to relieve pain, which may also hasten death. Advance directives are also available through the society so that patients can document their wishes for future medical treatment.

France has a national health care system with a well-developed hospice care program. The system is funded through contributions by employees and employers. Employees donate about 6 percent of their income, while employers contribute almost 13 percent. All contributions go exclusively toward medical care. Other payroll deductions are taken for additional social services, such as retirement. Patients pay for medical service when it is rendered and are then reimbursed by the government after submitting the proper forms. Prescriptions are also funded, in varying amounts, depending on type of medication; generally, the government pays 70 percent of the cost, and individuals often carry a supplementary health insurance policy that covers the rest. France's high average life expectancy rate of seventy-eight years reflects its superior health care and the advanced state of medical technology typical of an industrialized society. The high quality of health care coupled with an excellent hospice system for managing extreme pain may contribute to lack of official concern for the legalization of euthanasia and physician-assisted suicide.

France may also reject the notions of euthanasia and physician-assisted suicide because of traumatic events in its recent history. Although France was an ultimate victor in World War II, the country was devastated by German occupation. Germany not only left scars on the land, it also marred the images of authority figures, political leaders, and physicians. French physicians may hesitate to be associated with the concept of euthanasia (voluntary or involuntary) or physician-assisted suicide because of the fear of social stigmatization through past abuses of the handicapped, the deformed, the elderly, and non-"Aryan" individuals. And this fear may extend beyond the medical community, into the general population. Seeds were planted regarding the horrible consequences of out-of-control authority and unchecked political power. While these doubts may be barely noticeable in the younger generations, it may still take a substantial period of time for them to fade into obscurity.

5

Euthanasia in Australia, China, Japan, and India

Australia

From July 1996 until March 1997, for the first time in history, euthanasia and assisted suicide were practiced both openly and legally in the world. In the Northern Territory of Australia, terminally ill patients could seek to prematurely and voluntarily end their lives with the assistance and guidance of a physician. It is not at all surprising that the law had its origins in this crocodile-infested, sparsely populated, rugged area that is twice the size of the state of Texas. The Northern Territory has been self-governing since 1978 and has enjoyed a reputation as a trailblazer, often asserting itself through maverick, rebellious tendencies and legislation. A prime target of this free-spirited and free-thinking region is the Australian federal government. Although the federal government is among the largest employers in the region, Territorians remain highly antagonistic toward being told what to do by outsiders.

The History behind the Law

In February 1995, Marshall Perron, head of the Northern Territory government, introduced the most liberal euthanasia legislation the world had ever known. The reasons behind his decision to author such a bill are still somewhat unclear, but Perron is said to have been influenced by a "collection of life experiences" and the deaths of his mother and his close friend.[1] Perron denies writing the euthanasia bill for personal gain or notoriety and maintains that he resigned his government position the morning the euthanasia debate began because he did not want the vote to be influenced by that position. Some observers of the debate, however, claim that he resigned in order to sway undecided votes to his side. The final vote in the parliament was a close thirteen to twelve.

Perron still searches for possible flaws in the legislation but, nevertheless, remains convinced that the legislation was appropriate. He believes the safeguards built into the legislation were more than adequate to protect against any abuses. "An important thing to remember is that medical technology has allowed us to become so good at keeping people alive that it's reaching a stage where just about everyone will die with someone else making the decision. Why can't the patient make that decision instead?"[2]

The Rights of the Terminally Ill Act of 1995

Perron's legislation, the Rights of the Terminally Ill Act, was enacted into law on May 25, 1995, and came into effect on July 1, 1996. The act's purpose was to "confirm the right of a terminally ill person to request assistance from a medically qualified person to voluntarily terminate his or her life in a humane manner; to allow for such assistance to be given in certain circumstances without legal impediment to the person rendering the assistance; to provide procedural protection against the possibility of abuse of the right recognized by this Act; and for related purposes."[3] The act had stringent guidelines that had to be met before assistance to die would be provided.

Most patients did not utilize the law (as predicted by many opponents) due most likely to the several steps that had to be taken to fully ensure that they qualified for the procedure and possibly because the federal government decreed that no health funds could be allowed for euthanasia procedures. The act also stated that attending physicians were free to refuse the request for assistance to die. Patients then had to locate a physician who was willing to comply with their wish to die, which could be a lengthy process, outlasting the course of the terminal illness. If patients were satisfied with the palliative care treatment being provided, assistance to die was not granted. But if the physician was not qualified to provide adequate palliative care treatment, then information had to be given to the patient by a physician who was qualified.

Physicians could help patients die if a series of provisions were met. The most basic requirements were that patients had to be at least eighteen years of age, terminally ill, and experiencing extreme pain and suffering. A second, independent physician, specializing in the terminal illness of the patient, had to also examine the patient and confirm the diagnosis and prognosis. A psychiatrist had to further examined the patient to determine that the patient was not suffering from a treatable clinical depression. Physicians had to be convinced that patients were fully informed about other options, mentally competent, and had made the decision without any coercion by family, loved ones, or other medical personnel. In addition, physicians had to be satisfied that patients had thought about the implications for their families of their deaths. During this process, patients could rescind their request at any time. The guidelines called for a cooling-off period of at least seven days from the time an informed verbal request was received by the physician from the patient until the "certificate of request" was signed and witnessed. There was another forty-eight-hour waiting period before the request was carried out. Assistance offered to patients included prescribing, preparing, and either giving the lethal substance to patients for self-administration or administering it for them. The physician remained with the patient until death occurred and then reported the death to the authorities and documented it in the patient's medical records.

The Case of Robert Dent

On September 22, 1996, the first legalized euthanasia death occurred—of cancer victim Robert Dent. Since this pivotal event, the country has been divided by several emotionally charged disputes among religious, political, and local activist groups.[4] Supporters of euthanasia hailed Dent as "an ordinary man with the extraordinary courage to shorten his own life" and a "pioneer and a fighter who gave his life to the cause he believed in."[5] Detractors, on the other hand, "deplored euthanasia as murderous and immoral" and prophesied that "it will be a short step to justifying the taking of a life that is no longer productive."[6] A representative of the Roman Catholic Church stated that the euthanasia law is "nothing short of murder."[7]

Dent suffered from incurable prostate cancer that had progressed so far that he could not even receive a simple hug for fear that his ribs would crack. Dent died with the assistance of Dr. Phillip Nitschke, a leading advocate of voluntary euthanasia who resides in the Northern Territory. Dr. Nitschke developed a computer program that activates a dose of lethal drugs to the patient. Before the drugs are administered, a set of questions is posed designed to ensure that patients know exactly what they are doing. For instance, one of the prompts reads, "This device has been set to deliver a lethal injection. To proceed to the next step, you must press 'yes.' If you press 'yes,' you will cause a lethal injection to be given in thirty seconds and you will die. Do you wish to proceed?" The individual can cease the proceedings at any time during the course of the event.[8]

Dent foresaw the reaction to his death by opponents of euthanasia and wrote an impassioned letter the day before he died describing his painful and unsuccessful medical treatment since 1991. He said, "The Church and State must remain separate. . . . What right has anyone, because of their own religious faith (to which I don't subscribe), to demand that I behave according to their rules until some omniscient doctor decides that I must have had enough. . . . If you disagree with voluntary euthanasia then don't use it, but don't deny me the right to use it if and when I want to."[9]

Public Opinion Data

A September 1996 Morgan poll revealed that 76 percent of the respondents believed a hopelessly ill patient who requests a lethal injection should be given one. The responses were based on the question, If a hopelessly ill patient, experiencing unbelievable suffering, with absolutely no chance of recovering, asks for a lethal dose, so as not to wake again, should a doctor be allowed to give a lethal dose or not? This poll confirmed the pro-euthanasia sentiments Australians have held since 1946. The significant difference appears to be that a majority favor active euthanasia, as opposed to passive euthanasia, indicating that individuals want to play a role in the decision-making process of their own deaths.[10]

The Centre for Human Bio-Ethics at Monash University conducted surveys in 1987 and 1993 of the Australian medical community in Victoria. The results showed that approximately 60 percent of the respondents answered yes to the question, Do you think it is sometimes right for a doctor to take active steps to bring about the death of a patient who has requested the doctor to do this? Further, almost 50 percent of the physicians reported that they had received a request from a patient for death to be brought about more quickly, and of that 50 percent, close to 30 percent said that they had fulfilled the request. Over one-half of the physicians who refused the request did so because the act was illegal. Almost 60 percent of all those questioned in the survey were in favor of changing the law to allow voluntary euthanasia in certain circumstances and under certain conditions.[11]

In 1992, the same research team examinedthe attitudes of almost 2,000 nurses from the state of Victoria on identical issues. The situation is different for a nurse than a physician in that the physician prescribes the treatment course for the patient and it is the nurse's duty to carry out the treatment. In other words, the nurse has more personal contact with the patient and may be called upon to make ethical judgments that conflict with professional responsibilities. When asked, In the course of your work has a patient ever asked you to hasten his or her death (whether by withdrawing treatment or by taking active steps to hasten death?), 55 percent responded that they had; the primary reason for a patient requesting euthanasia was "persistent and unrelievable pain." Sixty-six percent of the nurses reported having been asked by a patient to stop providing life-sustaining treatments; 10 percent complied with the patient's wishes without obtaining permission from the attending physician first. Twenty-five percent of the nurses had been asked by a physician to participate in an action that would result in ending the life of a patient who had requested euthanasia; 85 percent of the nurses reported complying with the request.[12]

In 1994, the School of Community Medicine, University of New South Wales, conducted a mail survey of physicians in New South Wales and the Australian Capital Territory to determine their attitudes toward both active and passive euthanasia and their actual practice of both. Nearly 50 percent of the physicians reported that they had been asked to perform euthanasia. Of this group, 28 percent stated that they had complied with the patient's request. In those cases in which the patient requested that the physician assist with a suicide, 7 percent of physicians reported that they had followed the patient's wishes. Physicians in this survey favored euthanasia at levels only slightly lower than that reported repeatedly by the population at large.[13]

The Australian Medical Association is officially opposed to legalizing voluntary euthanasia in spite of evidence that shows substantial support among practicing physicians. But it has endorsed the patient's rights to passive euthanasia and to receive pain-reducing medication, even if the treatment might shorten the patient's life. The legality of its position is based on intention: if the intention of the pain medication is to reduce pain, then the act is considered legal under common law.

Between May and July 1996, a study was funded by the National Health and Medical Research Council to compare the proportion of medical end-of-life decisions in Australia with that of the Netherlands. The survey was a self-administered questionnaire given to 3,000 randomly selected active medical practitioners located throughout Australia. Nearly 2 percent of all deaths that occur in Australia are the result of euthanasia or physician-assisted suicide. In almost 4 percent of these deaths, involuntary euthanasia (death without the patient's explicit consent) was practiced. Of these cases, 38 percent of the patients had some discussion with the physician regarding hastening death, but no explicit request was made. In almost all of the remaining instances, the physician did not consider the patient to be competent. Nearly 25 percent of all Australian deaths resulted from a decision not to provide treatment to the patient, with the specific intention of accelerating death. In 7 percent of the deaths, physicians used opioids as part of the treatment for two purposes: to relieve pain and suffering and, by administering a large enough dose so as to be fatal, to effect death. In almost 37 percent of all deaths, physicians made medical decisions to end the lives of patients by hastening death in some manner. Physicians from the Netherlands made comparable decisions in close to 20 percent of all deaths.[14]

Other Right-to-Die Laws in Australia

In Western Australia, under common law, the patient has the right to refuse medical treatment, and the state government is currently considering a bill that would make the common law right fully recognized and provide terminally ill patients the right to refuse medical treatment. In Queensland, no laws exist that require individuals to accept medical treatment, nor do any laws state that an individual can refuse medical treatment. In Victoria, the Refusal of Medical Treatment Act of 1988 allows persons to utilize their common law right to refuse unwanted medical treatment. In New South Wales, physicians are permitted to discontinue life support on the basis of clinical judgment and in consultation with the patient's family.

In South Australia, a person of sound mind and over the age of sixteen has the common law right to refuse medical treatment, a right extended by the Natural Death Act of 1983. The Natural Death Act was supplanted by the Consent to Medical Treatment and Palliative Care Act of 1995, which allows patients to determine their level of medical and life-sustaining treatment. In Tasmania, a physician is not allowed to actively assist patients to commit suicide, but again, patients have the right to refuse treatment. In the Australian Capital Territory, the Medical Treatments Bill of 1994 provides patients the right to refuse treatment and permits life supports to be switched off. It further guarantees access to pain relief even if it can cause death.[15]

Since the death of Robert Dent, euthanasia legislation has been hotly debated. The Morgan poll found that 71 percent of the respondents believed the government should not override the Northern Territory's law on euthanasia. Only 19 percent of the respondents believed it should be revoked.[16] The Northern Territory's euthanasia law came under attack by both the Federal Parliament and the High Court. Kevin Andrews, a Liberal backbencher from Victoria, introduced a euthanasia bill, which sought to outlaw euthanasia. In addition, the Andrews bill (as it is usually referred to) seeks to change the Northern Territory Self-Government Act so that the Northern Territory (as well as the Australian Capital Territory and Norfolk Island) would not have the power to pass voluntary euthanasia legislation, although the states would still be able to. Subsequently, the Northern Territory's voluntary euthanasia law would be rescinded. Because the Australian Federal Parliament does not maintain equivalent power over the state parliaments, any euthanasia law passed in the future by a state could not be revoked and could spark a constitutional challenge on the question of whether a commonwealth law supersedes a territory law, as opposed to a state law.[17] The Andrews bill did not retroactively punish any physician involved in a euthanasia act while the legislation was in place.[18]

On November 18, 1996, the opponents of the Northern Territory's euthanasia law applied to the High Court of Australia for "special leave" to appeal the decision of the Northern Territory Supreme Court that found the Northern Territory Parliament had the power to make the law and that it was made validly. The High Court adjourned the application for special leave to appeal the decision of the Northern Territory Supreme Court, stating that it would not hear the issue while a bill was before the Federal Parliament to override the territory's legislation. If the Federal Parliament bill passed, then no law would exist for the High Court to consider. In early December, the Andrews bill passed the lower house, but it had yet to pass in the Senate. Until such time, the law could not be put into effect.

In February 1997, the Roy Morgan Research Centre conducted a survey that revealed that 77 percent of the voters in Kevin Andrews's district disapproved of Andrews's objective of overturning the Northern Territory's euthanasia law and that nearly 80 percent of the respondents were in favor of a terminally ill patient's right to ask for and obtain a lethal dose of a drug from a physician.[19] In March the final debates on the Andrews bill were heard. Supporters of the Northern Territory's euthanasia law said they were up against "religious zealots," while the supporters of the Andrews bill hurled accusations at the supporters of the Northern Territory law of being Nazi war criminals.[20] The Northern Territory's euthanasia law was struck down by a vote of thirty-eight to thirty-three. An amendment was attached that required increased funding for palliative care treatment.[21] Citing public opinion data that showed the majority of Australians favored voluntary euthanasia, opponents of the decision urged other Australian states to pursue the passage of their own euthanasia regulations.[22]

In Summary

The euthanasia debate in Australia has been tumultuous. Four terminally ill individuals took advantage of the Northern Territory's law while it was in effect. Others were stranded in midprocess without a legally sanctioned right to have assistance in dying. Dr. Nitschke has been quoted as saying he never had aspirations to spend his whole life being a crusader for the euthanasia cause and that the whole situation has taken its toll on him both personally and professionally.[23]

The legalization of voluntary euthanasia in the Northern Territory of Australia is a reflection of the somewhat unconventional territory, coupled with social factors representative of the country as a whole. As a self-governing region, the Northern Territory has acquired a reputation as nontraditional and trendsetting. The territory's government passionately resents interference in running its government and drafting social legislation. But commonwealth power supersedes that of any territory. Thus, the Northern Territory is self-governing within limits, while the states retain greater governing power. It has been predicted that some of the Australian states will introduce their own euthanasia legislation. If state legislation passes, the commonwealth does not have the authority to overturn it as it did in the Northern Territory, and a domino effect may follow.

The religious sector both within the country and abroad has also expressed strong opinions about the euthanasia law in the Northern Territory. Cardinal Edward Clancy, the head of the Catholic Church in Australia, in addressing the issue of euthanasia stated that "it has two names, either murder or suicide" and characterized the Northern Territory's law as "arrogant and irresponsible."[24] Cardinal Clancy appealed to the community to support an attempt to overturn the law. On an international scale, the Vatican fueled the moral debate by calling the euthanasia law and the surrounding events a "new monstrous chapter in the history of humanity."[25] The head of the Anglican Church and the archbishop of Melbourne held that there was imminent danger that the voluntariness of euthanasia would ultimately turn into "subtle pressure" to choose euthanasia, especially when the patient becomes a burden to the family. The archbishop further stated that it is a slippery slope when weighing economic factors against a life that is no longer considered socially productive.[26]

Interestingly, when only religious persuasion is considered, every major denomination in Australia clearly favors euthanasia.[27] In a 1995 Morgan poll, the percentages favoring euthanasia by religious persuasion were Anglican, 84 percent; Methodist, 93 percent; Presbyterian, 85 percent; Roman Catholic, 66 percent; United Church, 84 percent; those with no religious preference, 90 percent. It appears, however, that in the end religious authority wielded greater power than religious practitioners in influencing political decision makers on the moral pitfalls of euthanasia, as opposed to the benefits of relieving pain and suffering and granting the individual a death with dignity. Church leaders remain strongly instrumental in crafting social policy in Australia.

Like most other industrialized nations, Australia boasts a long life span for both men and women. Australia operates under a national health care system, which some have criticized as becoming increasingly institutionalized in the area of primary care. [28] Since health care is nationalized, the system is not market driven by physicians and medical institutions, thus it is not subject to ever-increasing costs for goods and services, as is the case in privatized systems such as in the United States. The Australian health care system does not provide any coverage for physician-assisted suicide or voluntary euthanasia. Hospitals throughout Australia already regularly practice passive euthanasia by terminating life-support-system assistance or by withholding food, water, or antibiotics. Support for passive euthanasia by all Australians has consistently remained close to 70 percent in this decade, according to Morgan polls. With most other medical expenses paid for by the government, no economic incentives exist for the medical community or loved ones to compel the patient to consider euthanasia or assisted suicide. In the sense that gaining an inheritance is viewed as an economic benefit or incentive, this could unfortunately always be a motive in persuading the patient to elect a premature death through euthanasia.

The passage of the world's first euthanasia legislation is attributable to the unique factors that characterize the Northern Territory of Australia and other aspects that are inherent in the country. The Northern Territory had the legislative will to construct and enact the euthanasia law because of its no-nonsense, matter-of-fact approach to individual autonomy. In a sense, the region extrapolates its views on itself as a territory to the individual as a member of society: the Northern Territory regards itself as autonomous and self-determining and as separate from the states and the other territory of Australia. In addition, Australia is a prosperous industrialized nation with an advanced, nationalized health care system, so individuals live longer, healthier lives and have access to superior medical facilities and treatment. But extended life spans do not always translate into acceptable lives, especially during the final stages of a terminal illness such as cancer, which can be intractably painful. Individuals with access to advanced health care are often disillusioned when they face the situation of surviving longer but under unhappy conditions.

China

The Chinese government has been extensively involved in population control measures. This has resulted in the adoption of the one child per family policy and in exploration of end-of-life processes. In 1994, surveys were conducted on the public's attitude toward euthanasia. The Zhong Xinwen She agency reported that there was more than a 70 percent approval rate in support of euthanasia.[29] In 1995, the National People's Congress received a draft bill advocating the legalization of euthanasia and specifying conditions under which euthanasia would be allowed: euthanasia would be performed only in urban hospitals, the patient's relatives would have to provide consent in the form of a verified letter, and the procedure would have to be approved by a minimum of two experts. The dual purpose of the bill was to minimize suffering and to allow patients to die in a dignified manner.[30] Passive euthanasia remains a complicated topic, as the Chinese lack a definition for brain death.

At the other end of life's spectrum, China has passed a law, supposedly directed at improving the quality of births, that prohibits individuals from having children if they have serious hereditary and or contagious diseases. China has also implemented (though not rigidly) the one-child-per-family rule, which has been in effect since 1979. Government officials also promote delayed childbirth and, after one child has been born, encourage parents to submit to either sterilization, to prevent future pregnancies, or abortion of any subsequent pregnancies. Government policy dictates the prominent role of the medical professional in these practices. The physician's decision in matters of death through euthanasia or limitations on childbearing appears to be binding. To further increase chances that the individual will abide by these regulations, the Chinese government provides single-child families with income incentives, priority school enrollment, health care, employment, and housing benefits. In a surprising move for a country that assumes marriage to be a normal part of every adult's life, the government has further endeavored to control population growth through the suggestion that some individuals should not marry at all.

The status of health care and sanitation have improved dramatically since the 1950s, with many major epidemic-producing diseases such as cholera and typhoid having been wiped out. Life expectancy has more than doubled in this time period, currently peaking at seventy years of age. Unfortunately, the incidence of cancer, cerebrovascular disease, and heart disease has risen, making them some of the leading causes of death in China. Due in part to economic reforms, China attempted to privatize the collective medical care system in the 1970s but reasserted control over the program in 1990. The government is faced with escalating health expenditures due to the increased life expectancy rate after the containment of diseases that routinely killed thousands, the advent of medical technology trickling into the rural communities, and the prolonging of life for those with new, lingering, costly terminal illnesses such as cancer. The utilization of euthanasia for the terminally ill could be part of the country's solution to capping health care costs.

Due to the changing structure of the traditional family, the government is also feeling the strain of having to provide more services and care for its elderly population. The traditional family is evolving into something more nuclear in nature. Households have generally subsisted by pooling their incomes, with the standard of living for the family dependent upon the number of wage earners. Family size is closely associated with class, with government officials and rural landlords able to support the largest families and peasant farmers the smallest. The least economically advantaged segment of the population, the landless peasant laborers, sometimes cannot afford to marry and begin families.

The requirement to provide for the elderly and the relation between number of sons and familial economic success have encouraged nontraditional family units to develop over time. The family structure plays a twofold role as both an economic enterprise and a domestic network. In contemporary society, the three-generation family provides the perfect solution for the wage-earning second generation, with healthy grandparents providing child care for the third generation. The entire family also benefits if the elder member retired from a state position, which allocates a pension and above-average housing to those retirees. This situation is not so ideal if elder members are unable to care for themselves. In the past, the family has been bound both legally and customarily to support and care for their disabled and elderly members. Currently, the state guarantees assistance when the family cannot adequately sustain these individuals.

Japan

Until recently, death and dying were considered taboo or inappropriate subjects for discussion in Japan. This cultural practice of nondiscussion is readily discernible in the health care field. It is common practice for a physician not to disclose to terminally ill patients the true nature of their condition or a prognosis of impending death.[31] To further complicate the situation, it is highly unusual for the Japanese to question those in authority, such as physicians, or to even express their opinion regarding their medical situation. When physicians actually have discussed their patients' medical situations, many patients describe the physician's manner as "mechanical" and "insensitive."[32] The fact that the average time the physician spends with the patient is approximately two to three minutes supports the policy of nondisclosure about medical conditions. This brief encounter would not leave time for human compassion and empathy or for a thorough explanation about the immediate course of treatment, curative expectations, or palliative care options.

The failure to reveal truthful information to patients' on their conditions has implications for the euthanasia debate as well. If patients are unaware of their actual medical diagnosis and prognosis, then in all likelihood the practice of euthanasia would be of an involuntary, nonconsensual nature.[33] Death in this situation would be viewed as a mercy killing, not as voluntary euthanasia. The Japanese tend to think of euthanasia more as refusal of treatment than as acceleration of death through such means as a lethal dose of narcotics, either administered by a physician or self-administered. *Songen-shi* refers to a dignified death after the loss of reasoning capabilities or faculties and the onset of severe pain. This is usually thought of as a death occurring without taking extraordinary or unnecessary measures. *Anraku-shi* is a direct translation of euthanasia, meaning a good death. The Japanese generally believe that this form of death is somewhat hedonistic in that it is performed solely to circumvent the pain of the illness.[34] These beliefs are reflected in the advocacy agenda of the world's largest euthanasia organization (75,000 members), Japan's Society for Dying with Dignity, which was founded in 1976. The organization does not directly lobby for the right to voluntary euthanasia, involuntary euthanasia, or physician-assisted suicide. Its main goal is to formally legalize death with dignity by allowing the removal of life-sustaining equipment and the refusal of life-extending treatment in the final phases of a terminal illness.

Influential Case Histories

Two cases illustrate the growing concern of a densely populated society hesitant to openly discuss death, coupled with an aging population faced with ever-increasing prolongation of life through advanced medical technology. Both of the cases triggered heated ethical, medical, and legal debates within Japan. In the spring of 1991, Dr. Masahito Tokunaga, working at Tokai University, administered a fatal injection of potassium chloride to a terminally ill, late-stage lung cancer patient. Previous to the injection, the family had made repeated, persistent requests to relieve the pain and suffering of the patient. The physician finally submitted to the family's wishes and was charged with the murder of his patient. In 1995, the court handed down a two-year suspended sentence to the physician.

The court justified the sentence on the grounds that the patient's family had reiterated their request on several occasions and also on the grounds that no guidelines existed in Japan for coping with this type of situation. The court stipulated four conditions under which mercy killing would be permitted in Japan: the patient's acceptance that death is inevitable and imminent, the patient's clearly stated wish to hasten death, unbearable physical pain, and the absence of any other course of treatment. A follow-up study to this case, conducted by a psychiatrist at Tokai University on the attitudes of physicians and psychiatrists to euthanasia and suicide, demonstrated that physicians essentially supported Dr. Tokunaga's actions, two-thirds adding only that they would have adjusted the timing of the patient's death by increasing the dose of opioids and would have explained the ramifications of the mediation to the family.[35]

In April 1996, Dr. Yoshihiro Yamanaka, director of a hospital in Keihoku, Kyoto Prefecture, injected a lethal dose of a muscle relaxant into a cancer patient without the patient's consent to euthanasia or knowledge of the procedure. This action was taken because the patient had not died after a purportedly lethal dose of morphine was administered. At no time was the patient ever told he had cancer or was expected to die soon. Dr. Yamanaka maintained that the patient's wife asked him not to artificially extend the life of her husband. The police became aware of the event after receiving an anonymous telephone call. Dr. Yamanaka admitted to performing euthanasia on several patients within the last decade in response to a patient's family's requests to do so. In June, Dr. Yamanaka took a three-month leave of absence from the hospital and upon his return in September was reassigned to the position of chief researcher. In response to this case, one physician stated, "The Kyoto 'mercy killing' case is the epitome of what is wrong with the medical system in Japan. It shows that a doctor stands in a position of authority that is far above the patient and this leads to the doctor failing to see the humanity of the person he is treating."[36] The case has yet to be resolved.

Public Opinion Data

A Mainichi Shimbun survey on the attitudes of heads of hospitals about euthanasia and death with dignity showed that nearly one-half of all physicians treating terminally ill patients have received a request not to prolong a patient's life. About 15 percent stated they might not comply with the guidelines set by the 1991 ruling because many patients are not informed that they have cancer and the decision is therefore made by family members.[37] In October 1996, a newspaper poll showed that 70 percent of physicians approved of euthanasia and slightly more than 70 percent favored mercy killing, provided the patient consents; 63 percent supported the right of the patient to withdraw from medical treatment or to seek a death with dignity.[38]

Social Considerations

Japan's opposition to euthanasia and physician-assisted suicide seems to be more a function of its unique cultural traits than the traditional religious objections commonly found in other countries. Japan is primarily a secular society, in which developing integrated, agreeable relationships with others through reciprocity or social obligations is deemed more important than the individual's connection or interdependence with a transcendent divine power. The idea of individual autonomy is subsumed to social collective considerations in the pursuit of greater social harmony. An individual's choices in life and death ultimately have ramifications for the entire group. Because of Japan's strong social cohesiveness, its culture is grounded in a powerful collective identity and solidarity, emphasizing the tradition of cooperation. Social interaction is based on harmony, order, and the self-development of the individual, with beliefs about the self and its relationship to society drawn from many philosophical and religious traditions. The culture reinforces the notion of working together and the interdependence and interrelations that must develop for this effort to be successful. From the earliest moment of one's life, the family is the focal point for the individual's introduction to social development and organization. The family provides a strong social support network throughout life and during the dying process.

Other cultural and demographic concerns also affect Japan's response to euthanasia and physician-assisted suicide. Japan is the most densely populated country in the world in terms of arable land per person, with a population of nearly 125 million in an area only 150,000 square miles. It is three times more densely populated than Europe and twelve times more densely populated than the United States. By the end of the twentieth century, it is estimated that Japan will have one of the highest percentages of senior citizens in the world, with life expectancy topping eighty years of age. Unlike in many Western countries, in Japan the elderly hold a position of status, prestige, and respect. Customarily, elderly individuals reside with grown sons or daughters and continue to play an active part in their families. But there has been a growing trend for the elderly to maintain separate households away from their families. Like many countries, Japan faces the financial problems of a rapidly increasing elderly population with extended life spans brought about by advanced medical technology. Government spending on social welfare programs is predicted to increase by a factor of at least four by the year 2025. This strain on the government is due to escalating expenditures for pension plans, increased demand for health care by the elderly, more expensive treatment for lingering, chronic illness, and the costs associated with medical care throughout a prolonged terminal illness. This drastic increase in the elderly population could push Japan to review its policies on social spending and the treatment of the aged, terminally ill patient.

The health care system in Japan is a combination of public and private programs. Health care costs are met through a combination of private insurance company funds and government-sponsored programs. For the most part, employers provide comprehensive medical insurance through an employee benefits program. For those who are unemployed or lack adequate income, government medical insurance covers the majority of the expenses. The elderly receive medical care free of charge.[39] As Japan is one of the leading economic powers of the world, with an average per capita income of almost $18,000, most individuals have access to health care treatment.[40] Thus, with health care insurance benefits provided by either the individual's employer or the government, few economic inducements exist to use euthanasia duplicitously to save medical care or personal funds.

India

India is a country rife with contradictions regarding the concept of death. Legally, attempting or assisting suicide is strictly prohibited. However, India's dominant faith, Hinduism, sanctions and promotes suicide for certain moral and social reasons, although other Indian religions would preserve all life without exception. Indian attitudes toward life and death are also strongly influenced by the segment of society of which they are a part—urban or agrarian, high or low caste. Suicide is practiced openly in India with a religious or moral imperative but not in the context of euthanasia or with physician assistance.

Euthanasia and physician-assisted suicide are not sanctioned by either the medical community or official legal doctrine. Part 3 of the Indian Constitution specifies the basic rights granted to the Indian citizen, and Article 21 further elucidate these rights, stating "No person shall be deprived of his life or personal liberty except according to the procedure established by law." While there is no expressed or implicit restriction on individuals giving up their lives of their own free will or accord, Article 21 pertains only to the deprivation of life or personal liberty by the state and not by the individual. The Indian *Penal Code,* Section 309, says that attempting to commit suicide and the assisting of suicide (under Section 306) are both punishable by imprisonment. Successfully committing suicide is not considered a crime, but the attempt may result in imprisonment.

India's legal and ethical treatment of death is full of incongruities. Although the law specifically forbids killing a person via euthanasia, physician-assisted suicide, or self-induced suicide, it is legal to abort a pregnancy under the Medical Termination of Pregnancy Act of 1971 (Act 34). Act 34, which permits the ending of a pregnancy by a licensed medical practitioner under certain conditions, was purportedly a response to the population explosion in India, as demonstrated in Section 3 (2)(b) of Explanation II: "Where any pregnancy occurs as a result of failure of any device or method used by any married woman or her husband for the purpose of limiting the number of children, the anguish caused by such unwanted pregnancy may be presumed to constitute a grave injury to the mental health of the pregnant woman." The law allows for the deliberate termination of an unwanted life, with the decision-making power residing with an individual, whose life will not be taken, on the basis of her emotional trauma. Yet with regard to euthanasia and physician-assisted suicide for the terminally ill, individuals experiencing excruciating physical pain and trauma are not legally allowed to decide to terminate their lives.

Religious Considerations

In India, religious practices regarding death and illness, which might seem to contradict the law, are often practiced openly and without legal recrimination. While the taking of the life of a terminally ill individual through euthanasia or physician-assisted suicide is strictly prohibited by law, the age-old custom of *sate* or *suttee* (the practice of healthy women who choose to prematurely end their lives on the funeral pyres of their husbands because of moral, social, and religious dogma) has been performed in India for hundreds of years without hesitation. Contracting an illness or disease is another common reason for committing suicide. In this instance, the act is performed not so much to avoid pain and suffering as to avoid social disgrace and isolation. In the past, a stigma of shame attached to those who had a disease or illness, and suicide was thought to be preferable to living with the stigma.[41] Even though euthanasia and physician-assisted suicide are not legally sanctioned, many cases exist in which sick individuals commit self-sacrifice by drowning, walking into the wilderness, or other harsh means.

Ancient religious beliefs and tenets play a significant role in structuring society's contemporary response to death and the dying process. Hinduism, through its caste system, profoundly affects the social structure of India. As in almost all other world religions, God (Parama Brahma) serves as the creator of humankind, and it is through his will that individuals are granted life. Individuals are expected to comply with God's wishes and to forgo life in his name and honor. In the Hindu Vedantic philosophy, death is by no means the end of life: it represents only the physical death of the body. The astral body (consisting of one's life experiences, intelligence, etc.) continues in existence on the astral plane and eventually in the heavenly plane, where it is intermingled in the Ocean of Energy and the Eternal Parama Brahma. Through God's will, the astral body is placed into another physical body in conjunction with the individual's previous deeds. Life and death are thus cyclical, with death signaling the beginning of a new life, not the end of an existing life.[42] According to Hinduism, everything inevitably disappears in life, and it is expected that death occurs many times with great pain and suffering.

While Hinduism has historically promoted the sanctity of life and strong family values, it has also taken a lenient attitude toward some forms of suicide. Suicide is acceptable for such reasons as disgrace, shame, dishonor, political tyranny, and the death of a loved one. But hastening the end of life for a terminally ill individual would be incompatible with the supreme being's divine plan. The tenets of Hinduism do not directly devalue human life, but the religion does demonstrate its tolerance of suicide through its strong reverence for the afterlife.[43] Historically, some members of the highest Hindu caste who were qualified for the priesthood (Brahmins) have committed suicide by self-starvation for the sole purpose of reaching a state of perfect bliss known as Nirvana. Suicide by self-starvation is considered permissible in India and is still widely practiced, as is suffocation by holding one's breath.

In comparison to Hinduism, Jainism is intolerant of any form of killing for any reason. Jains are a much smaller segment of the population than Hindus. Jainism requires that five sacred vows be taken, among which are the vows to not willfully destroy any life and to contain one's necessities such that living things are not destroyed unnecessarily.[44] Strictly practicing Jains go so far as to walk lightly on the ground in order not to kill insects.[45] Abstaining from killing or doing harm are fundamental beliefs of Jainism and are the basis for all their moral prescriptions. All rules of social behavior are founded on this concept, and Jainism specifies that life not be destroyed unless it is absolutely necessary to do so to sustain a higher life. If terminating life is required for this purpose, it must be done with the least possible harm.

Social Considerations

In addition to religious considerations and legal restrictions that oppose the performance of euthanasia and physician-assisted suicide, other social indicators are influential in shaping India's response to death and the dying process. India has an extremely closed social system because of its caste system. In this caste system, there is almost no chance for social mobility, as one's position in life is based on ascriptive characteristics, over which one has no control. Although the caste system was dramatically adjusted through legislative means in the

1950s, it continues to exist in a modified form. An individual's caste determines many of life's fundamental decisions, such as occupation, marriage partner, social acquaintances, social activities, place of residence, and access to health care treatment.

Although India has a national health care system, not everyone has access to it because of the area they reside in, discrimination against the lower castes, and lack of medical training, equipment, and supplies. Almost 80 percent of India's one billion citizens reside in small, remote villages, largely a function of the location of the agricultural jobs they hold.[46] Traditionally, agrarian peasants adhere to the time-honored customs of their ancestors and shun modern-day developments. In these villages, industrial technology is all but absent, and a high population density further contributes to increased rates of disease and infection, unsafe living and working conditions, exposure to untreated waste, extreme poverty, and hunger. These deleterious living conditions and lack of modern medical technology have contributed to poor health and have effectuated a shorter average life span, with the typical Indian living only fifty-nine years.

Many Indians are simply concerned with subsisting from day to day, rather than with the possibility of dying. Powerful family ties and established social traditions provide a network of support for the individual. This web of social support allows for the distribution of food, health care for the ailing, and assistance for the elderly when needed. This network assumes many of the responsibilities that social service organizations normally do, including caring for the dying.

6

Euthanasia in Colombia, South Africa, Iran, and Israel

Colombia

Colombia, South America, is the only country in the world in which euthanasia is a legal medical option for terminally ill patients who give clear consent to the procedure. Before the sanctioning of euthanasia by the nation's Constitutional Court in 1997, the civil law was not explicit with regard to euthanasia but addressed the issue in Article 26, Homicide for Pity, which stated that when an individual killed another for pity, to end the other's intense suffering from a corporal wound or incurable illness, a prison sentence of six months to three years would result. When developing the law, the legislature avoided the term *euthanasia* and hence the action was referred to as a homicide. Euthanasia was penalized in an inflexible manner, but judges could impose the least restrictive punishment if they felt it was justified.[1] When the court was asked to consider the issue of euthanasia after a number of mercy killings in the country, the Bogota attorney Jose Euripides Parra Parra, who had originally raised the issue, actually sought to toughen the penalties.

The Constitutional Court of Colombia has a liberal history in many areas of lawmaking, including decriminalizing the possession of small amounts of narcotics and imposing prison sentences on a spouse who forces the other to perform sexual acts. This court stands out as somewhat of an anomaly in such a conservative country (public discussion of euthanasia is virtually nonexistent in other Latin American countries). It came as no surprise to many that on May 20, 1997, the Constitutional Court, with the power of judicial review, decriminalized voluntary euthanasia for the terminally ill under the conditions that written consent is clearly and precisely provided by the patient and that the consent is given under noncoercive conditions. The ruling does not apply to chronic or degenerative conditions such as Alzheimer's or Parkinson's disease; the condition must be considered terminal—such as cancer, kidney failure, and the final stages of AIDS. The court further struck down the mandatory prison sentence of six months to three years for anyone involved in a mercy killing. But the court did not establish guidelines for the process, saying that lawmakers, not the court, should set the standards for physicians to follow.

On June 12, 1997, the court ratified its May 20 decision and has asked the Colombian Congress to develop a set of guidelines under which mercy killings are legally permitted. The speculation is that the Congress will not take immediate action, for many reasons, including a crowded legislative agenda and the low priority of euthanasia for Colombians. As of this writing, no guidelines have been introduced. Some observers have hypothesized that the guidelines will be so restrictive that the practice of euthanasia will become too difficult and cumbersome to attempt. For instance, the Congress could require that the physician/patient relationship be one of some predetermined period of time. While such a relationship may be common in the Netherlands, it is not so in Colombia, because citizens who participate in a state-sponsored prepaid health plan are assigned various physicians, so it is nearly impossible to establish a long-term relationship with any one of them. Health care services are provided by the public sector (which covers approximately 65 percent of the population), the social security sector (which covers slightly more than 22 percent of the population), and the private sector (which covers nearly 13 percent of the population). The private sector consists of prepaid health plans and is relatively new. Access to health care can be difficult. Although the system is designed so that a medical facility is no more than two hours' walking distance from anywhere in the country, the majority of medical personnel are concentrated in urban areas.[2] The average life expectancy of a Colombian has recently risen to seventy-two years.

The legalization of euthanasia in Colombia has generated a storm of controversy in a country that is predominantly Roman Catholic. Church officials have implied that the justices supporting the decision to legalize mercy killing have forsaken valuing human life and have eroded social values. The church has requested that the euthanasia law be immediately revoked on the grounds of the traditional Catholic doctrine of sanctity of life and individual spiritual growth through suffering. According to the Reverend Candido Lopez, "by his faith, the Christian is called to unite his sufferings with those of Jesus of the cross. It is through the cross that Jesus works our Salvation."[3] The church is a powerful influence in the country, but it is too early to predict the effect it might have on the euthanasia ruling, including congressional development of guidelines or a total rescission of the law. During the court's hearing of the euthanasia debate, the justices voiced their respect for Catholic doctrine but held that individuals with alternative views and opinions are constitutionally protected. The court's president, Antonio Barrera Carbonell, said, "The state has the duty to protect life, but this duty is not absolute, it has a limit. There is not just one morality. Every person can determine their own sense of life, whether it is sacred or not."[4] It could take several years for the ruling to be fully utilized, but in the interim justice might turn a blind eye, as it does with abortion clinics, which are tolerated but remain illegal.

South Africa

In 1961, the Republic of Africa severed its ties with the United Kingdom and became politically independent, largely the result of differences over apartheid. As Black resistance to apartheid increased, the Caucasian sector resorted to brutal military repression. By 1986 a nationwide state of emergency was imposed as a result of increasingly violent protests. Former President F. W. de Klerk ended the state of emergency, lifted the ban on antiapartheid political parties (including the African National Congress), and released political prisoners, including the African National Congress leader Nelson Mandela. Apartheid laws were repealed in 1991, and negotiations began between de Klerk and Black leaders, leading to the establishment of an interim government and a new constitution. De Klerk's objective was to retain the Caucasian minority political domination while allowing for Black political participation. Subsequently, national elections were held, and Nelson Mandela was elected president in 1994.

Suicide is not criminalized in South Africa provided that no other ancillary assistance is given, but euthanasia and physician-assisted suicide remain illegal even in the case of mercy killing.[5] The patient does maintain the right of informed consent, which is common law in South Africa, and has several rights under the informed consent clause, including the right to refuse specific medical treatment even if the refusal will hasten death or cause injury. In addition, treatment may not be administered by a physician without the patient's consent, except in cases of medical emergencies or when there is a statutory duty to act. Treatment provided against the patient's wishes is considered an assault under common law. The patient must be mentally competent to give consent, and the consent must be based on provision of accurate knowledge about the nature and effect of the intended treatment.[6] The patient also has the right to retract treatment decisions previously made. If the physician refuses to comply with the newly stated treatment wishes, a new physician can be retained by the patient. Under informed consent, the patient's treatment decisions in matters of cessation or continuation always subjugate those of the next of kin or spouse.

SAVES, the Living Will Society (formally known as the South African Voluntary Euthanasia Society), was instrumental in getting the South African Law Commission to develop a discussion paper on euthanasia and related concerns. Originally, the society called for the formal legislation of living wills, but it was recognized that the scope of the project needed to be expanded to also include active and passive euthanasia.[7] In early 1992, the commission agreed to the project, and in 1994 it published its first working paper and called for comments. A wide range of responses was received, representing many diverse viewpoints. On April 15, 1997, the South African Law Commission issued its 100-page discussion paper titled, *Euthanasia and the Artificial Preservation of Life*. Again the commission asked for comments and will ultimately make suggestions to Parliament after its final report is complete. The paper is intended to establish the foundation for developing new regulations on euthanasia and physician-assisted suicide.

With respect to refusal of treatment, the commission reaffirmed the common law stance and stated that all competent individuals over the age of eighteen may refuse life-sustaining treatment. The refusal must be given freely of the patient's own accord, even if this decision may hasten death.[8] In terms of pain management, the commission recognized the problem of the double effect. When a terminally ill patient's pain and suffering cannot be relieved through ordinary palliative treatment, the physician may increase the dosage of medication to provide relief even if it has the secondary effect of shortening the life of the patient.[9] The commission also described the conditions under which a physician may render assistance in dying through euthanasia or physician-assisted suicide to the competent patient over the age of eighteen. The most obvious condition that must be satisfied is that the patient has a terminal illness that has been confirmed by an independent practitioner. The patient must also be experiencing extreme suffering, and euthanasia must be the only medical option remaining that will relieve the pain. The patient must further be properly informed about the terminal illness, its prognosis, and the treatment options available, and the decision to end his or her life must be an informed and well-thought-out decision. The request for assistance in dying must be persistent, but the decision may be negated at any time by the patient without repercussions. The request may be fulfilled only by a medical practitioner, but no medical practitioner is obliged to assist.[10] In this situation, the patient may seek another physician's assistance.

Iran

Suicide and euthanasia are strictly forbidden by Islamic law, and euthanasia (active or passive) is considered murder.[11] The law also states that a murderer will never have the right to an inheritance or bequest from the deceased regardless of the motivations for the murder (noble or otherwise, intentional or unintentional). Euthanasia is prohibited because it assumes that God does not have the ability to perform miracles for the terminally ill and it interferes with God's dominion over life-and-death matters. Islamic tradition holds that the body is not owned by anyone, and thus one is not free to choose what to do with it. Islamic law even prohibits praying for death to come, as God is the only entity with the power to make decisions about death. Death is an event the individual should face with courage.

In the case of a terminal illness, death is considered an expression of God's will, and the patient should rejoice in the fact that only a select group is chosen by God to face the test of suffering. Islamic law maintains that the punishment for committing suicide to avoid pain is to endure the suffering caused by the suicide instrument (knife, poison, etc.) eternally in hell. The individual will be denied access to paradise and the respect granted to the dead. If the individual had assistance in the act of suicide, the assistant will not be granted any of God's mercies either. Suicide is considered legitimate, however, in situations where one is defending a religious cause or if the worshiper is experiencing an unbearable religious ordeal.[12]

The practice of euthanasia or physician-assisted suicide is considered religiously unlawful in the Islamic culture. Sanctity of life is decreed by God, and the individual is created by God and entrusted by him to care for, nurture, and protect his or her body. Human life is to be respected unconditionally, regardless of other circumstances, such as terminal illness, pain, and suffering. Islam holds the individual responsible for his or her deeds while on earth. Those who live an obedient life will be aptly redeemed in heaven, and disbelievers will suffer the fate of an unending punishment.

Iran is directed by the body of law known as the Shari'ah. The Shari'ah consists of the Koran and the Sunnah, which the court follows to adjudicate cases falling within the guidelines of the religion. In matters of life and death, the court is authorized by both the community and the Shari'ah to determine if the cessation of life-prolonging treatment for a terminally ill patient is appropriate. An example of such a case would be a comatose, paralyzed, irreversibly brain-damaged accident victim. The court will listen to testimony from at least two medical experts on the prognosis for recovery of the victim. The court will also consider the suffering (emotional) and welfare (economic) of the patient's family, as the family's support is critical in these types of situations. Financial burdens imposed on the state are taken into account, because treatment in these severe cases is extremely expensive, and the court must weigh expending resources on this particular patient as opposed to one with a better prognosis. Essentially, the court attempts to secure public rights, or the rights and well-being of the entire state, as opposed to that of the individual.[13]

The state of the health care system in Iran is not adequately advanced to properly care for the population and is reflected in the relatively low life expectancy of sixty-seven years of age. The country continues to experience a high infant mortality rate as well. The primary causes of death include parasitic, gastrointestinal, and respiratory diseases. The Iranian Medical Association reports a shortage of all types of medical professionals, further complicated by the fact that the existing personnel are disproportionately distributed in urban areas. The family plays a large role in the life and death of a sick individual, and religious law bolsters the sanctity of the family in order to protect its inherent integrity.

Israel

Israel's population consists of 80 percent Jews and approximately 14 percent Arabs, the large majority of whom are Muslim (most of the rest are Druze). Religious concerns are paramount in all discussions of life and death in Israel. Judaism holds that only God has the power to grant and take away life. Every breath of human life up until the final extinguishing moment is held to be sacred, with existence in any state "superseding living the good life."[14] Accordingly, quality-of-life issues are always supplanted by the sanctity of life and the Halachic imperative to preserve life. Preserving and extending life should be the primary motivation in the medical decision-making process. In addition, patients have a duty to care for their own health and life. Preservation of life takes precedence over biblical tenets in all situations except cases of idolatry, murder, and incest.[15] In many instances, quality-of-life choices may be perceived as "nothing less than sanctioned euthanasia."[16] When treatment is considered futile or likely to increase the suffering of the patient, the patient is permitted to refuse medical treatment.

In spite of religious tradition, the Israeli Society for the Right to Die with Dignity was established in 1987. The goals of the society are to "respect the wish of terminal patients to die peacefully, without medical interventions which prolong a person's life without regard to the quality of life" and "promoting legislation which will confirm one's 'Living

Will' and will release doctors from legal responsibility."[17] In July 1994, the Knesset (the legislative body of the state of Israel) approved an amendment to Paragraph 34 of the *Penal Law*, 5737–1977, which states in part that "a person shall not be criminally liable for an act committed" when "the act was done to an individual with that individual's lawfully provided consent as part of a medical procedure or treatment whose effect is the benefit of that individual or another." The amendment entered into effect in July 1995. The society hopes that this amendment will assist in confirming the living will of the patient. In 1996, a clause that was supposed to elucidate the issue in the Patient's Rights Law was deleted, most likely because of pressure from the religious community. The society apparently prefers ambiguity to clarity, as clarifying the law would directly contradict Halachic beliefs.[18]

Within the Jewish ethical tradition, the question of the acceptance or rejection of euthanasia and assisted suicide is framed slightly differently, but the interpretation process results in answers to the same fundamental issues. In Judaism, abstract moral principles are usually converted into questions of legal obligation or responsibility. The inquiry is not whether an individual has a *right* to do X (for example, to die or to have an abortion) but rather what an individual is *obliged* to do in a given situation. For example, the questions considered within a Jewish-perspective right-to-die debate are: What are physicians attending terminally ill patients permitted to do in terms of precipitating death or ceasing intractable pain? If physicians assist patients to die, are they legally liable? What are terminally ill patients obliged to do?

Although the Talmud does not explicitly prohibit or forbid suicide, there is a high level of agreement in the Orthodox Jewish tradition on the repudiation of active euthanasia and assisted suicide. Perhaps this is due in part to the seemingly universal consensus on the subject in well-known works of literature by post-Talmudic scholars.[19] In Jewish law, the preservation of life is placed above all else, and accelerating death in any manner or being the direct cause of another individual's death is considered murder.[20] (The exception to this is the act of martyrdom. In this case, sacrificing one's life is considered a duty.) Controversy and confusion come from the meaning and translation of the phrase "direct cause." It is most often interpreted to mean that death must occur as a result of natural causes, not as a result of a direct act of a physician.

Passive euthanasia for a terminally ill patient is permitted under certain circumstances within the Jewish tradition, as the Talmud implies that the physician does not have to do everything possible to keep the terminally ill patient alive. Removing artificial means that are keeping a patient from dying, such as a feeding tube, is not considered a positive or direct action in that no element, such as a lethal dose of morphine, is introduced to cause death. The patient essentially dies from natural causes (for instance, starvation or dehydration), not from a positive action the physician undertook to induce death.[21] Under Jewish law, the physician or family does not have an obligation to pursue this path, but it is allowable in particular conditions. Thus, although there is an obligation to prolong natural life to the greatest extent possible, there is no legal obligation to prolong life artificially. Another interesting aspect of medical treatment guidelines is that in instances in which revealing the truth to the patient could precipitate a mental or physical setback in recovery, the physician should never divulge the true nature of the condition. If it is unlikely that the patient will benefit in any manner from this knowledge, then under no circumstances should he or she be told of the terminal medical condition.[22]

7

Toward a Workable Social Policy

Overview

Death has been the muse of religions, of philosophy, of political ideology, of artistic creation, and most recently, of advanced medical technology. To examine death divorced from its sociocultural milieu would be meaningless. Endeavoring to die prematurely is not solely the product of the progress of medical science. Requests to hasten death also rely on the prevailing moral and political atmosphere of a society. As religion and religious institutions began to lose their guiding moral authority in society, laws piloting the conduct of individuals gradually grew more secular in nature, recognizing individual choice and personal freedoms. Laws have progressively become a reflection of an increasingly pluralistic society, embracing diverse ideologies, convictions, mores, and beliefs.

The intensely private act of suicide has been occurring since the beginning of time. What is different about suicide in contemporary society is the attempt to position it and euthanasia under the management and guidance of the medical community in accordance with directives issued and authorized by the government, thus involving others in what used to be a personal matter. The issue has evolved from a self-inflicted death to one that requires the assistance of others because of life-prolonging medical treatments and aggressive drug therapies that have succeeded in keeping patients alive for a much longer period of time than previously possible. This sometimes results in intense, lingering pain, a low quality of life, or a condition in which the patient is unable to control basic biological functions such as eating, walking, urinating, swallowing, and breathing. Some patients are physically unable to commit suicide without professional assistance because they are too ill, confined to a hospital bed, cannot find someone willing to assist because of legal ramifications, or cannot stockpile the required amount of drugs to successfully accomplish the act.

Society has traditionally held that it is intrinsically wrong for one individual to provide assistance to another to commit suicide or to participate in a mercy killing, even when benevolent reasons exist to do so. Worldwide, legal systems rarely sanction the killing of another individual for any motive, mercy notwithstanding. The universal exceptions to this rule are cases of self-defense, capital punishment, and warfare. Patients, fearing the loss of control over their own final destinies, are demanding greater autonomy in the medical decision-making process regarding the timing and circumstances of their own deaths. In addition to having the legal right to refuse medical treatment, which in itself can contribute to needless pain and suffering (such as the slow, often agonizing process of starving to death), patients seek the ability to end their lives quickly and in a dignified and painless manner through either euthanasia or physician-assisted suicide. Public support of euthanasia and physician-assisted suicide is growing, and it rests on an appeal to compassion and mercy for those who are suffering and an affirmation of individual rights about end-of-life decisions. Autonomy is a fundamental principle in decision making about medical treatment. It is inherently connected to individual freedom and the ability to advocate on behalf of one's own best interest. The medical community should respect the patient's personal, moral, and religious beliefs when considering medical treatment options and approaches.

Historically, death was primarily caused by disease or accidents as a result of living and working conditions and lack of medical technology. When the medical and pharmacological sciences were in their infancy, the problem of unnecessary prolongation of life did not exist. The mistaken assumption was often made that longer life expectancies and declining death rates indicated that the population was becoming generally healthier. This assumption has been challenged, as evidence has revealed that extended life spans are accompanied by increases in chronic diseases (as opposed to acute illness) and disability. Acute conditions, such as smallpox, have a rapid onset, and their duration is relatively limited. These types of disease are either cured in a short period or they kill the individual. In the twentieth century, the medical community has been fairly successful in containing these diseases or eradicating them. Chronic illnesses, on the other hand, such as heart disease and cancer, can be managed but usually not cured. An increasing number of individuals are simply living longer with, and eventually dying as a result of, chronic conditions.

The gradual emergence of chronic diseases worldwide as the primary cause of death, coupled with the development of medical technology excesses, has given rise to a new accent on patient rights and other end-of-life decisions. Now, patients who are irreparably brain damaged, permanently comatose, or terminally ill are subject to the adverse side effects of the artificial extension of life due to medical advancements. (The beginning of life has also experienced the joys and consequences of this technology. Infants born with previously fatal afflictions and disabilities can be kept alive and sustained for months, if not years.) While sophisticated medical technology has lengthened life to its outer limits, which may very well be in accord with the universal desire for continued existence, it has also protracted the time that chronically and terminally ill patients must suffer pain and indignity. Is this extended life for terminally ill, seriously debilitated, or permanently vegetative individuals hooked to yards of tubing, respirators, and pacemakers worth the agony and the emotional, physical, and economic costs? Many believe that it is not and would prefer to be spared this unnatural existence through euthanasia or physician-assisted suicide. The wondrous benefits derived from medical technology, such as life-extending treatment, organ transplantation, and in-vitro fertilization, have also compelled society to look at its most basic values and human relationships. Society must come to some acceptable resolution concerning the proper use and direction of this new technology or face the consequences it brings.

Many patients mired in drawn-out suffering from a terminal illness, existing in a drug-induced stupor in an attempt to control pain, want the personal right to control the circumstances of their own deaths. This brings into question the societal setting, in which the focus is generally on the greatest good for the greatest number. Expressing these concepts in statutes can be perilous and difficult to contain and has socioeconomic, legal, and moral dimensions. Three concerns loom above all others: (1) whether and to what degree individuals have the right to control the ending of their lives within the context of their society; (2) the nature of the relationship between patients and their assistants in suicide; and (3) the resulting consequences for society.

Predictors of Right-to-Die Attitudes and Regulations

Right-to-die issues are emotionally charged and subject to moral debate, theological scrutiny, and ethical analysis. They have long suffered an unfortunate stigma from the political reign of Adolf Hitler and his use of the term *euthanasia* for his racial purification schemes and his bid for the genetic cleansing of Germany to rid it of the aged, the disabled, the diseased, and the deformed. Opponents thus fear that euthanasia and physician-assisted suicide could potentially discriminate

Table 7.1 Social Indicators, Euthanasia and Right-to-Die Regulations, Twenty Countries

Country	*Type of Legal System*	*Type of Health Care System*	*Public Opinion*	*Dominant Religion*	*Type of Government*	*Life Expectancy Age*	*Status of Law*
Argentina	Mixture of United States and West European legal systems	Public/private health care system	Not available	Roman Catholic	Republic	72 (68-M; 75-F)	Euthanasia and physician-assisted suicide illegal
Australia	Common law	Public health care system	High	Protestant/ Anglican	Federal multiparty parliamentary state with sovereign monarchy	76 (74-M; 81-F)	Euthanasia previously legal; currently illegal, with legislation pending
Brazil	Based on Roman Codes	Public/private health care system	Note available	Roman Catholic	Federal republic	62 (57-M; 67-F)	Euthanasia and physician-assisted suicide illegal
Canada	Common law	Public/private health care system	High	Roman Catholic	Federal parliamentary state with constitutional monarchy	77 (73-M; 80-F)	Euthanasia and physician-assisted suicide illegal

China	Civil law	Collective medical care system	High	No official religion (Taoism/Buddhism/ Confucianism)	Communist	70 (68-M; 71-F)	Euthanasia illegal but previously considered for legalization; physician-assisted suicide illegal
Colombia	Civil law	Public/private health care system	Not available	Roman Catholic	Republic	72 (69-M; 75-F)	Euthanasia and physician-assisted suicide legal
France	Civil law	Public health care system	Not available	Roman Catholic	Republic	78 (74-M; 82-F)	Euthanasia and physician-assisted suicide illegal
Germany	Civil law	Public/private health care system	Not available	Protestant	Federal republic	77 (74-M; 80-F)	Euthanasia illegal; physician-assisted suicide legal
India	Common law	Public health care system	Not available	Hinduism	Federal republic	78 (75-M; 81-F)	Euthanasia and physician-assisted suicide illegal
Italy	Civil law with ecclesiastical law influence	Public health care system	Not available	Roman Catholic	Republic	78 (75-M; 81-F)	Euthanasia and physician-assisted suicide illegal

Table 7.1—continued

Country	*Type of Legal System*	*Type of Health Care System*	*Public Opinion*	*Dominant Religion*	*Type of Government*	*Life Expectancy*	*Status of Law*
Iran	Based on Islamic law	Public health care system	Not available	Shia Islam (Muslim)	Thocratic republic	67 (66-M; 69-F)	Euthanasia and physician-assisted suicide illegal
Israel	Based on a mixture of common law/ British mandate regulations/4 basic laws enacted by Knesset	Public health care system	Not available	Judaism	Republic and parliamentary democracy	78 (76-M; 80-F)	Euthanasia and physician-assisted suicide illegal
Japan	Civil law	Public/ private health care system	High	Shintoism/ Buddhism	Constitutional monarchy	80 (77-M; 82-F)	Euthanasia allowed if guidelines are followed
Netherlands	Civil law	Public health care system	High	Roman Catholic/ Protestant	Constitutional monarchy	76 (74-M; 81-F)	Euthanasia allowed if guidelines are followed

Russia	Civil law	Public health care system	Not available	Russian Orthodox	Federation	69 (64-M; 74-F)	Euthanasia and physician-assisted suicide illegal
Spain	Civil law	Public/ private health care system	Not available	Roman Catholic	Parliamentary monarchy	77 (74-M; 80-F)	Euthanasia and physician-assisted suicide illegal
South Africa	Based on Roman-Dutch law and common law	Private health care system	Not available	Christian	Republic	60 (57-M; 62-F)	Euthanasia and physician-assisted suicide illegal
Switzerland	Civil law	Private health care system	Not available	Roman Catholic	Federal republic	79 (75-M; 82-F)	Euthanasia illegal; physician-assisted suicide legal
United Kingdom	Common law	Public health care system	High	Anglican	Constitutional monarchy	77 (74-M; 79-F)	Euthanasia illegal, physician-assisted suicide legal
United States	Common law	Private health care system	High	Protestant	Federal republic	76 (72-M; 79-F)	Euthanasia illegal; physician-assisted suicide legal in Oregon

against those individuals in society who have less of a voice in determining social standards and guidelines for appropriate behavior, who lack the income for adequate health insurance and medical treatment, and who may be considered a burden on society (such as the permanently institutionalized, the aged, the disabled, and the ill).

Some countries burdened with population-control problems have implemented extreme measures, such as limiting the number of children a family can have. Concern abounds that euthanasia and physician-assisted suicide could be used in such countries not so much for humanitarian reasons as for managing their expanding populations and to lower the costs of providing health insurance, disability pay, and retirement benefits. One of the greatest fears about the legalization of euthanasia and physician-assisted suicide are actions taken for economic reasons by health insurance companies that do not want to continue to pay for expensive, aggressive treatment for a terminally ill patient whose fate has already been determined; by families of patients that stand to gain an inheritance or relief from future medical expenses; and by hospitals treating uninsured, terminally ill patients who are not going to live to pay the bills. For these and other reasons, consensus is not easily achieved, and regulation of euthanasia and physician-assisted suicide is not uniform in countries around the world.

Opponents also contend that individuals are indebted to society for their existence and must perform certain social duties in return for the overall benefits that society provides them. By taking one's life, a person is reneging on this commitment as a functioning member of society. In addition, the practice of euthanasia and physician-assisted suicide go beyond the individual in that the participation of another party (by either the actual commission of the act or by providing the patient the means for completion of the act) turns the death into a social consideration and must, therefore, adhere to the norms, standards, and laws established by the community. Whereas suicide used to be considered a purely individual act, it has become a social act because of the requirement for assistance by the terminally ill.

It is difficult to discern why euthanasia and physician-assisted suicide regulations exist in some countries and not in others. It is even more difficult to define specific social indicators that determine why standards or regulations range from making euthanasia legal or quasi-legal, or illegal (see table 7.1). But some general conclusions can be drawn.

First, in those countries where euthanasia or physician-assisted suicide are (or were) legal, there appears to be a trend toward self-determination, or the right of the individual to control the course of his or her own life. It assumes individual autonomy in choices concerning the self as long as these choices do not injure or endanger others.

Allowing individuals to control the nature and circumstances of their deaths would permit patients with a terminal illness to die in a dignified manner and to prevent extended suffering when quality of life has dwindled to zero. For many individuals, it is the quality of life that is important, not the quantity or sanctity of life.

Second, in all but one of the countries in which either euthanasia or physician-assisted suicide is practiced or has been practiced, civil law is the basis of the legal system. In civil law, which has its foundation in Roman law, the primary legal rules are embodied in a central code, which the courts apply to the case at hand without reference to previous decisions, which is the tradition in common law. Typically, a civil law system is thought of as more restraining and conservative than a common law system due to its predefined legal code. In addition, civil law is not adversarial in nature, as is common law, thus allowing for a different type of statutory evolution to take place. When specifications do not exist in the code to appropriately examine the case at hand, some courts have taken it upon themselves to develop guidelines. Other courts have simply circumvented the code and drafted conditions under which euthanasia and physician-assisted suicide can be performed. While the acts are not formally legalized, they are only prosecutable if the guidelines are not followed.

In the Netherlands, for example, euthanasia and physician-assisted suicide are technically not allowed by statute, but since 1973 there has been a gradual series of judicial steps authorizing physicians to practice euthanasia and physician-assisted suicide if they adhere strictly to the guidelines provided. Development of policies regarding end-of-life decisions in the Netherlands stems from a unique understanding of contemporary social problems and the devising of creative approaches to their resolution. The laws, it is believed, should incorporate several different ideologies, doctrines, and philosophies to accommodate an ever-evolving society. Similarly, in Japan the court system issued a set of conditions under which mercy killing would be permitted. This was done because the courts believed that there were inadequate direct specifications for coping with the cases being brought before them. In Colombia, the Constitutional Court, in a somewhat surprising move, legalized euthanasia when it was originally asked only to consider the issue of increasing the punishment associated with the crime. The court has a long liberal history in many areas of lawmaking concerning individual rights, including the controversial decision to decriminalize the possession of small quantities of drugs. The court, which is viewed as the most progressive and liberal in South America, has asked the Colombian Congress to assist in developing guidelines. Thus, both the judicial system and the legislature will be involved in the legalization of euthanasia.

The exception to civil law and pro-euthanasia laws is Australia. In the Northern Territory, the legislature took the lead in crafting and enacting a euthanasia law. The law reflects how the territory is viewed in relation to the country as a whole—trailblazing, free spirited, and rebellious. Even though polls revealed that the law enjoyed the overwhelming support of those outside of the region, it was eventually overturned by the Australian Parliament, which supersedes the territory in legal decision-making authority.

Legislatures have also been instrumental in promoting individual rights associated with dying through inaction. By not enacting statutes that specifically prohibit a practice, governments have essentially sanctioned that practice. An interesting scenario is developing in the United States. The Supreme Court was asked to rule on two combined right-to-die cases. In its decision, the Court did not determine that there was a constitutional right to physician-assisted suicide, but neither was the act declared unconstitutional. The right to die had previously won voter approval, in Oregon in 1994, but had been tied up in the courts on appeal ever since. Polls showed that a majority of Oregonians still favored legalization of physician-assisted suicide, and a heavy voter turnout was predicted. The attempt to repeal physician-assisted suicide was unsuccessful, and Oregon became the first state in the United States to legalize the act. This situation has been closely monitored and is considered a watershed event for the country's right-to-die movement. Several states, including Michigan and Hawaii, are expected to follow Oregon's lead. Again, the government in question is highly sensitive to self-determination and autonomy principles and may be instrumental in the passage of euthanasia or physician-assisted suicide legislation.

A third factor common to all of the countries that have implemented some form of right-to-die regulations is industrialization. Industrialization is a key reason that euthanasia and physician-assisted suicide are on the forefront of the social, political, and legal agendas of many countries. Industrialization has enhanced both living standards and progress in medical research and technology, and these have worked conjointly to increase life expectancy. But while there are apparent benefits in higher life expectancy rates and declining death rates, the repercussions are not all positive. Some of the most obvious consequences include rising costs of social welfare programs (including health, disability, and retirement) and artificially extended life spans, during which patients with a chronic or terminal illness may be subject to extreme pain and suffering.

Euthanasia and physician-assisted suicide provide one minor mechanism that many countries have explored to remedy what some may consider a negative consequence of increasing life spans. Subsequently, many approaches have been taken to legalize euthanasia and physician-assisted suicide. The most common justification for pursuing such regulation is, of course, to relieve the pain and suffering of the terminally ill. Very few countries have admitted entering the debate for other purposes, although perceived benefits beyond that of terminating pain and suffering are presumably weighed as well. Some countries have participated in the debate more fully than others. Those that have been virtually silent on right-to-die concerns have been so because of political turmoil, pressing social issues, religious considerations, or memories of historical use of "euthanasia."

Fourth, except for Switzerland, the countries with euthanasia or physician-assisted suicide regulations also have a publicly funded health care system. Health care is becoming increasingly important as the world's population expands and life expectancy rates rise. The key element in the euthanasia and physician-assisted suicide debate with respect to health care is economic. When individuals receive health care through the government, the financial burden on families is relieved. Therefore, the family has no financial incentive to coerce the patient into seeking euthanasia or physician-assisted suicide. (The prospect of family members receiving an inheritance upon the patient's death, however, is always a potential factor.)

The Netherlands is an example of what publicly sponsored health care can do. Its health and medical standards are among the highest in the world, with coverage for over 99 percent of its citizens. The Netherlands also stands apart from other countries in pain management for the terminally ill and the treatment of pain in hospices or hospice-type settings. Palliative treatment is extremely advanced, and care facilities are located adjacent to nearly every hospital.

Colombia and Japan provide health insurance to their citizens through a combination of publicly and privately funded programs. Privately administered health plans are a relatively new phenomenon in Colombia and consist of prepaid types of plans. In Japan, employers provide comprehensive medical insurance through an employee benefits program. For those who are unemployed or lack adequate income, government medical insurance covers the expenses. The elderly receive medical care completely free of charge, regardless of their circumstances.

Fifth, public opinion is another important aspect of right-to-die legislation. Opinion testing on euthanasia began with sampling of the general public and eventually expanded to those working with terminally ill patients—physicians and nurses. Survey data are not available on right-to-die issues in all of the countries discussed, but the data that do exist point to definite trends.

Attitudes have been tested on right-to-die issues since the early twentieth century in the United States and the United Kingdom. In the late 1930s, data from the American Institute of Public Opinion and Gallup showed support for mercy killing ranging from 39 to 46 percent.[1] During the same time, a poll conducted in the United Kingdom revealed public support at almost 70 percent.[2] By 1947, support for euthanasia by Americans dropped to approximately 37 percent when they were asked if a physician should be permitted to end the life of a patient if an incurable disease is present and either the patient or the family requested it. This decrease in support was probably the result of the atrocities that occurred in Germany and in German-occupied countries during World War II as a result of Hitler's "euthanasia" program. By 1973, 53 percent agreed, and by 1982, 61 percent said yes to the original 1947 survey question.[3] In 1994, Michigan respondents were asked which they would choose between prohibiting all physician-assisted suicide and legalizing it under certain criteria; 66 percent supported legalization. The same survey showed that almost 50 percent said they definitely would or probably would take advantage of the law if they themselves had a terminal illness.[4]

A 1996 poll in the United States reported a 75 percent approval rate for physician-assisted suicide. One year later, another survey showed an 80 percent approval rate for physician-assisted suicide, and over 80 percent of respondents stated they would support a family member's decision to choose suicide if he or she were terminally ill.[5] The United Kingdom has shown similarly high rates of approval. In a 1986–87 national survey, 75 percent of the respondents favored permitting physicians to end a patient's life when the patient had a painful, incurable disease. By 1996–97, the figure was 82 percent.[6] Another 1996 survey found that 80 percent of the respondents believed that human beings should have the right to choose when to die.[7]

Canadian polls have shown similar levels of support for euthanasia and physician-assisted suicide. In 1995, 85 percent of Canadians polled approved of terminating life-sustaining treatment for a competent patient who was unlikely to recover; 66 percent favored euthanasia under the same circumstances; and 55 percent believed that physician assistance was appropriate. In the situation of an incompetent patient unlikely to recover, 88 percent agreed to cease any life-sustaining treatment if the patient had previously expressed such wishes through a living will; 76 percent approved of removing such treatment from an incompetent patient based solely upon a request made by the family.[8] Gallup Canada and *Dying with Dignity, Canada,* conducted a survey in

1995 after the Special Senate Committee on Euthanasia and Assisted Suicide published its results; 75 percent of the respondents agreed that a physician should be allowed to end a patient's life if the patient has a disease that is life threatening and causes a great amount of pain and suffering. The patient must make a formal request for the mercy killing in writing. When the question was posed about a chronic illness (as opposed to a terminal illness), Canadians were not as supportive, but a majority (57 percent) still believed that it should be allowed.[9]

Chinese surveys also report high levels of support for euthanasia. The Zhong Xinwen She agency reported a greater than 70 percent approval rate for euthanasia in China. The rate of approval was similar when elders' responses were considered in isolation from the remaining sample population.[10] China has attempted to legalize euthanasia but thus far has been unsuccessful. In Australia, where euthanasia was practiced legally for a brief period, public support is strong. After the first legal death attributable to euthanasia in September 1996, the Australian Morgan poll revealed that 76 percent of the respondents believed a hopelessly ill patient who requests a lethal injection should be given one. This poll confirmed the pro-euthanasia sentiments Australians have held since 1946. The significant difference appears to be that a majority favor active euthanasia, as opposed to passive euthanasia, indicating that individuals want to play a role in the decision-making process regarding their own deaths.[11] In February 1997, the Roy Morgan Research Centre reported that 77 percent of voters in the district of Kevin Andrews (author of the Andrews bill) were strongly opposed to overturning the Northern Territory of Australia's euthanasia law and that nearly 80 percent were in favor of a terminally ill patient's right to obtain a lethal dose of a drug from a physician.[12]

Overall, medical practitioners tend to support euthanasia less enthusiastically than the general public. In 1964–65, nearly 50 percent of 2,000 general practitioners in England said that a dying patient had requested final relief from suffering; 36 percent said they would perform voluntary euthanasia if it were legally sanctioned.[13] In 1988, 35 percent of Colorado physicians reported giving pain medication with the effect of shortening a patient's life (whether intended or not), and 35 percent said they would be willing to administer a lethal dose if it were legal to do so.[14] In 1995, 60 percent of Oregon physicians felt that assisted suicide should be legal.[15] In 1994–95, 22 percent of Michigan physicians said they "might be willing to participate with either the patient or physician taking the final action."[16] In 1994, one out of every six physicians in Washington reported receiving a request for physician-assisted suicide; by 1995, that figure had increased to one out of every four.[17]

In Northern Ireland only about 20 percent of physicians supported physician-assisted suicide in 1997.[18] In Australia, however, 60 percent of physicians surveyed believed in taking steps to cause the death of a patient who requests it.[19]

In Japan, a survey showed that nearly half of all physicians treating terminally ill patients had received a request not to prolong a patient's life. About 15 percent stated they might not comply with the guidelines set by the 1991 ruling because many patients were not informed of their condition.[20]

Less strong support for the practices of euthanasia and physician-assisted suicide most likely result from several interrelated factors. First, purposely seeking the death of a patient is contrary to the Hippocratic oath that a physician swears to abide by. Even if death is imminent, precipitating death for the purpose of reducing pain and suffering is simply not acceptable to some physicians for moral reasons and personal concerns. The physician also faces organizational roadblocks. Neither the World Medical Association nor the American Medical Association support euthanasia or physician-assisted suicide. Both organizations sanction and ostracize any member practicing outside of their defined boundaries. Further, the physician and hospital stand to gain more by keeping the patients alive than by hastening their deaths. Medical research is expanded through the testing of medications, technologies, and treatment regimens, and medical practitioners become more experienced in treating terminal illnesses through caring for the terminally ill until a natural death occurs. In a purely economic sense, both the physician and the hospital benefit through the provision of costly advanced medical treatment. Ending a patient's life early reduces that compensation.

Sixth, relatively high life-expectancy rates are present in countries with euthanasia regulations, most likely due to industrialization, the advanced state of medical technology and pharmaceuticals, and access to sufficient health care made possible through the provision of health insurance. Religion does not appear to be a factor in whether regulations were present.

A Working Social Policy

If euthanasia and physician-assisted suicide are to be legalized, a law that accommodates the major concerns associated with the practices must be developed. The law is a formal method of social control that functions through the use of rules that are interpretable and enforceable by the courts within a political system. Social control is the governing of an individual's behavior in an effort to make that behavior congruent with the interests and expectations of society as a whole. Social control is required at the point at which human beings begin to reside together in a group environment. It serves to preserve order within society and adds the important element of predictability to social relations. While the overall goal of law is achieving social control, the law performs other functions as well. Its most common objectives include achieving public order, settling basic value conflicts, resolving individual disputes, setting rules, defining boundaries, and designating authority among government agencies. When drafting laws on euthanasia and physician-assisted suicide, the most important objectives are settling basic value conflicts and establishing rules and boundaries for the rulers (in this instance, the physician overseeing the patient's medical treatment).

Since value judgments underlie euthanasia and physician-assisted suicide concerns, conflicts are bound to emerge among religious groups, ethicists, vulnerable social groups, and others. In a highly advanced, complex society, different groups will have various opinions about appropriate and acceptable behavior. If these opinions strengthen to the point of conflict, it becomes necessary for the maintenance of social order that the differences be resolved. A primary function of the law, then, is to provide a means for peacefully settling basic value conflicts that exist within society among the many divergent social groups.

Gradually, as society evolves, some rules of behavior become law, while others do not. Some social norms are encompassed into formal codes through the judicial system; others are informally relegated to be embodied into coetaneous morals, manners, customs, and tradition. Which social norms actually become law is determined by several factors, one of the most fundamental being whether the norm contributes to accomplishing basic tasks within society, such as protecting persons and property. Another important factor is whether the law would reflect the commonly held values of the community. Those values most widely agreed upon, such as the belief that harming another individual is wrong, are the ones most likely to receive legal recognition. Concordant with this factor, it is important to determine the depth of feeling or sentiment about the issue in question. The issue behind these strongly felt norms and mores tends to be emotionally divisive. Recent examples of disuniting issues are abortion, the death penalty, and the legalization of marijuana for medical purposes.

Another significant consideration in determining if a widely held standard will become law is whether the issue demands uniformity in behavior so as to avert unintentionally dangerous conflicts. In this case, it is not the rightness or the wrongness of the act that is in question but its practicality. Under certain circumstances, legal standards have to be set that are applicable to the entire community for safety reasons. An example in the United States is requiring drivers of motor vehicles to drive on the right side of the road in order to avoid accidents. An important implication of this attempt to avoid potentially dangerous situations is the hazardous consequences of maintaining the sanctions against euthanasia. When safeguards are lacking, abuses of the procedure, such as euthanizing without obtaining consent from a competent patient or euthanizing according to some individual standards, will continue and will remain undetectable. This creates a less predictable and more unsafe situation than would be the case if the procedure was available legally and subject to strict scrutiny.

A last factor that is crucial in deciding whether a norm will be incorporated into law is if the proposed law would impose standards that would be too cumbersome or too costly to enforce or might be considered inappropriate, such as those involving privacy concerns with which the government hesitates to interfere. The legal system also has difficulty embodying social principles into law when moral or ethical standards conflict. Legislators are reluctant to incorporate into law an issue that has socially ambiguous, changing, or flexible standards. Oftentimes, the solution to this type of situation is to make the option legally available so that those individuals who view the act as morally acceptable can take advantage of the law, while allowing it to remain optional for those whose value systems do not accept it. A recent example can be found in the legalization of abortion. Some physicians believe that abortion is immoral, and they will not perform the procedure under any circumstances, even though the act is legal and accepted by others in the field without question. On the other hand, some physicians approve of abortion and are legally entitled to perform the service. The law allows for choice. The law functions to appease both parties in this manner. A similar approach is taken by many in the euthanasia and physician-assisted suicide debate.

Prevailing laws on euthanasia and physician-assisted suicide are contradictory, ambiguous, and shed little light on the appropriate course of action a physician should take in an already difficult situation. If euthanasia and physician-assisted suicide are ever to be fully legalized, a well-balanced law must be developed to address these concerns. All good laws contain certain broad principles and provide a framework that is flexible enough to cover any situation that might arise. Clearly, if euthanasia and physician-assisted suicide are to be legalized, many factors must be weighed and viewpoints considered in order to obtain a working social policy for right-to-die issues. A balance must be struck between individual civil liberties and social responsibilities. Euthanasia and physician-assisted suicide legislation cannot be connected to the particulars of a given patient's situation; instead, the law must attempt to integrate more general precepts to blanket the most likely situations the greater populace would encounter. Thus far, generalization to other cases has been a difficult feat for the judges who have heard mercy-killing cases that deal with the plights of individuals rather than the masses at large.

The specter of abuse occurs, of course, most often in nonvoluntary, nonconsensual euthanasia. Fear of the slippery slope issues abounds in conjunction with the dehumanization and desensitization of society toward certain groups of individuals who are thought of as an economic burden or less than contributing members of society and who are seemingly powerless against the greater forces of institutions and bureaucratic regulations. If euthanasia or physician-assisted suicide becomes a legal medical option, then lawmakers must address these concerns in a forthright, direct manner and prescribe strict guidelines so as to protect both the patient and society against its potential misuses. The law must consider the two extreme sides of the issue—one in which the patient is able to provide consent to euthanasia and the other in which the patient is not able to give consent. In the latter situation, the law must appoint a guardian, if one has not been previously selected through an advance directive. The guardian must reflect upon the patient's previously expressed wishes, including any advance directives, and the wishes of close family and friends and arrive at a decision in harmony with what the patient would have chosen.

Legalizing euthanasia and physician-assisted suicide has proven to be an extremely complex task, as demonstrated by the extensive, cumbersome guidelines developed in both the Northern Territory of Australia and the Netherlands. Execution of the act itself is not the difficult part; it is the safety precautions for the patient and society at large that must be taken previous to the act's commission that are hard to encompass in a law. It is nearly impossible for the law not to become labyrinthine due to the vast number of matters it must speak to and safety concerns it must address. Some of these issues include coercion by the family or physician for economic or emotional reasons, a true desire to die versus a treatable depression, adequate pain-management administration, unauthorized mercy killings, the availability of hospice care, and the receipt of an accurate diagnosis and prognosis.

Many specifications have been suggested as guidelines to serve as essential elements of any euthanasia and physician-assisted suicide law. All of the euthanasia and physician-assisted legislation thus far proposed have common threads. Some of the most frequently proffered stipulations include:

- The patient must be suffering from a verified terminal illness (defined as having less than six months to live) confirmed by two other experts in the field other than the attending physician.

- Full disclosure must be made by a physician from a position of neutrality (personally and professionally) regarding treatment options without pressure to select one over others.
- The patient's reasoning capacity must not be distorted by a treatable depression (some sort of a physician-patient relationship is desirable so the physician has an understanding of the patient's history and future medical treatment wishes).
- The request for euthanasia must be made by a mentally competent patient or the request must have been made through a legal instrument such as a living will at a time of mental competency.
- The request to die must be made repeatedly.
- It must be determined that the decision to die is based on the free will of the patient independent of coercive suggestions from family or the medical community.
- Waiting periods of reasonable length should be imposed between the different steps in the process (a period not too extensive, with consideration of the length of time calculated left to live and the current pain and suffering of the patient).
- A dialogue must exist between physician and patient when a treatment decision is rendered. The physician must understand the meaning of the request and respond with concern and compassion, ultimately accepting, but not encouraging, the patient's decision to opt for euthanasia.
- All avenues of pain management and palliative care treatment must have been explored to the fullest extent available to medical technology, leaving euthanasia or physician-assisted suicide as the last viable option to relieve pain.

Legalization has the added psychological effect for the patient of being a medical treatment choice if the pain becomes intolerable or quality of life has diminished to a point that the patient deems unacceptable. Fear of losing control and dying contribute to support of euthanasia and physician-assisted suicide. These fears stem from the failure of physicians to aptly apply technology. On one side, medical technology is overused to sustain life beyond its natural limits, forcing patients to confront unwanted, often painful treatments. On the other side, medical technology to relieve pain is greatly under utilized. Often, simply having the power to make this decision provides comfort and relief to the patient.

The medical community has managed to establish effective guidelines and standards of conduct for itself throughout its history. If guidelines for euthanasia and physician-assisted suicide are to be developed, the medical community must again play a fundamental part in providing an operating framework under which these medical treatment options could be administered. It is essential that pain management and palliative care be included in any treatment advisories and that a physician's first and foremost duty is to attempt to minimize any pain the patient is experiencing. The inability of medical researchers to cure chronic diseases requires a transformation of medical treatment priorities from curing to caring at a point when it becomes apparent that the patient has no genuine chance of recovery. Guidelines must also be clarified in the area of the double effect of pain medication administration. Physicians must be able to provide pain relief without the fear of prosecution and without the concern of drug addiction on the part of the patient. One way to alleviate this problem would be to allow the patient control of his or her medical treatment: direct control of pain relief with a self-administered opiod drip to the patient would remove the middleman in the treatment process. With effective pain management, the patient is less likely to request assistance in suicide or ask for a lethal injection. Finally, when a lethal dose of medicine is prescribed for purposes of euthanasia, those physicians writing the requests and those pharmacists filling the requests must not be subject to prosecution. In June 1998, Attorney General Janet Reno stated that the United States Justice Department would not use existing drug control laws to punish those involved in dispensing medication for euthanasia procedures.[21]

Advance directives can be part of the solution, as well. These allow individuals to write down their treatment preferences while they are still mentally competent and able to communicate them. Documentation of patients' medical care wishes provides a legitimate, verifiable method of making treatment decisions. The family is spared unnecessary emotional hardship, and expensive, unwanted, invasive treatment is avoided. When advance directives are not present, medical care providers assume that patients want everything possible done to preserve life, even if this means existing in a vegetative, artificially sustained state. Patients may have mistakenly believed that their wishes would be carried out through a spouse or relative, but in the absence of advance directives, the majority of medical personnel assume that all avenues of medical treatment must be utilized in keeping the patient alive. While advance directives offer some protection to the individual, very few are ever drafted, and even fewer are followed by medical personnel for several reasons: medical personnel are not aware of the existence of the directive, they fear a liability lawsuit, or their own value systems prevent them from carrying out the patient's wishes.

Changes in the health care system itself should accompany any changes made in the law. Euthanasia and physician-assisted suicide must remain the absolute last treatment option for the patient. Everything must be done to enhance the final months, days, and hours of terminally ill patients so that they are not forced to choose a premature death simply because pain management is not adequate or conditions have deteriorated to an unacceptable state. Improvements are required at all levels of the health care system. Health care professionals treating terminally ill patients need to adjust to the reality that not all treatments are going to be medically successful, and they must be willing to make the transition from curative treatments to palliative care. The definition of a successful treatment regimen must be reevaluated; good medical treatment need not always be defined as prolonging life to its furthest limit; instead it may be what is most humane, what serves to relieve pain, and what makes the patient feel most comfortable. When a competent patient has been refused euthanasia and is forced to undergo unwanted treatments, such as the invasive procedures of chemotherapy or attachment to a respirator or even less-invasive treatments such as the intake of oral antibiotics, the body has been invaded without consent, and under common law a battery has been committed. The patient should have the right to refuse such measures. Changes must also be made in long-term care institutions, in short-term care facilities, and among home-care service providers. Training, supervision, funding, and back-up support are key in these three areas.

Long-term care facilities (nursing homes) supposedly provide a place in which the elderly can spend their remaining days in comfort, in a secured environment, and under the guidance of trained medical professionals. They also serve as a staging ground for the elderly who are terminally ill. The task of locating such a facility that is both affordable and has available bed space is difficult. When the patient has behavioral problems, social adjustment difficulties, or severe physical disabilities, the task becomes next to impossible. Complaints about these institutions include deplorable and filthy living conditions, inadequate nutrition, poorly trained workers, neglect, murder, lack of respect, theft, injury, abuse, and other unthinkable, inhumane treatment. Many governmental incentive programs have been implemented in an effort to improve conditions, but most have met with little success. With the rapid increase in the oldest sector of the populace, changes will perhaps follow market demand rather than face legislative intervention.

Short-term, end-of-life care (hospices) focuses on pain management and comfort care, not curative treatments, for terminally ill patients. This type of care can be given in an institution or through a home-based situation. Opponents of euthanasia and physician-assisted suicide often suggest that hospice care is the solution for providing a supportive, caring environment for patients in their final days. Many advocates of euthanasia and physician-assisted suicide agree that if patients' pain can be controlled, most will not seek to hasten their deaths. But adequate pain management is very difficult to achieve and demands constant monitoring by medical personnel. Unfortunately, physicians and other medical professionals seldom receive enough training in pain management. They are also hesitant to prescribe enough medication to relieve pain due to unrealistic concerns about addiction or the fear of prosecution for overprescribing narcotics. Quality-of-life issues also arise in hospice settings. Patients may suffer side effects from their illness (incontinence, physical weakness, blindness) and from the pain medications (nausea and vomiting), or may be in a comatose condition because of the amount of opiods needed to control their pain.

An emerging problem with hospice care is that enough facilities simply do not exist to meet the demand, and there are often long waiting lists to get in, which, of course, is a significant problem when a patient has less than six months to live. Physicians often defer making a decision about transfer to a hospice facility until it is too late to get the patient committed before he or she dies. Further, the transition from curative, aggressive treatment to palliative comfort care is counter to the way many physicians think; ceasing treatment goes directly against what every physician is trained to do. In a sense, many physicians mistakenly believe they have been defeated or unsuccessful. Also, some physicians believe that informing the patient that further aggressive treatment would be futile and that hospice care may be more suitable will give the patient the message that the physician is giving up (when in reality the patient may be relieved).

Many terminally ill and elderly individuals are able to lead full lives in their own residences if adequate outside care is provided. Medicaid and Medicare encourage home care over institutionalized care when the situation permits. Home health care providers offer a wide range of services, including physical therapy and intravenous feeding, services that require professional training and expertise. In many states, however, home care training is severely deficient, and attendants operate under very little direct supervision while on assignment. Complaints abound concerning the unreliability and unprofessionalism of the attendants and about the improper, dangerous care they provide. Clients have been subjected to physical abuse, neglect, theft, and financial exploitation. Patients are often afraid to complain for fear of losing critically needed, sometimes life-saving, services.

The future course of end-of-life treatment greatly depends on training a growing number of health care workers. With the current trend of an increasingly older population in many countries, the demand for these types of workers may vastly exceed the supply. Obstacles for recruitment in these fields include low pay, little appreciation, stress, and a negative societal attitude toward the terminally ill and the elderly. With high workplace demands and extremely low pay, these positions sometimes attract individuals with questionable backgrounds and less than satisfactory health care experience. One report said that the employees of one long-term care institution consisted of "former mental patients, several men who had criminal records . . . people whose bizarre behavior seemed to indicate mental illness, and several men who appeared to be drifters in need of temporary employment."[22] The field needs to concentrate on better training, selective recruitment, increased pay and fringe benefits, and greater recognition for the importance of the work and its contribution to society. Finally, negative stereotypes against the sick, frail, and elderly must be combated and replaced with respect and compassion.

Conclusion

While medical technology has the capability to keep patients alive for a significant period of time (irrespective of quality of life), it also has developed similar capabilities to end life painlessly for those in agony. Still, these effective methods are shunned for more "natural" methods, such as starving to death. The Humane Society in the United States does not starve a dog or cat to death; it euthanizes the animal with a lethal injection, and the animal experiences a quick and painless death. Death row prisoners are not required to starve to death; they are given a lethal injection, and a biologically painless death ensues shortly thereafter. Yet society expects patients already in excruciating, unimaginable pain to end their lives in an even more distressful, undignified, painful manner.

The issues of prolonging lives through medical technology, lingering deaths, and an increasingly frail elderly population compel society to develop appropriate solutions for dealing with them. The amazing progress scientific medicine has achieved in the twentieth century has often been viewed only in a positive light. The adverse side effects of these breakthroughs also need to be examined. The new emphasis on the extension of biological life over the biographical component of life has caused many to forget that this is one of the primary distinctions between being human and being another life-form. For many patients, death is delayed past the point at which life is meaningful. As James Rachels held, "Generally speaking, death is a misfortune for the person who dies because it puts an end to his life. . . . Death is a misfortune, not because it ends one's being alive . . . but because it ends one's life."[23]

Notes

Chapter 1: Death and Dying in a Historical Perspective

1. Robert N. Bellah, "Religious Evolution," *American Sociological Review* 29 (1964): 358–74.

2. Robert M. Veatch, *Death, Dying, and the Biological Revolution* (New Haven: Yale University Press, 1976), 12.

3. E. A. Wallis Budge, trans., *Book of the Dead* (New Hyde Park: University Books, 1960).

4. Oscar Cullmann, "Immortality of the Soul or Resurrection of the Dead," in *Immortality and Resurrection*, edited by Krister Stendahl (New York: Macmillan, 1965), 9–53.

5. Derek Humphry and Ann Wickett, *The Right to Die: Understanding Euthanasia* (New York: Harper and Row, 1986), 3.

6. Aristotle, *Nicomachean Ethics*, vol. 5, chap. 11; Plato, *Republic*, translated by B. Jowett (New York: Van Nostrand, 1959), 297.

7. J. A. K. Thomson, trans., *The Ethics of Aristotle*, vol. 3 (New York: Penguin 1980), 130.

8. Plato, *Laws*, chap. 9, 873.

9. W. Mair, "Suicide: Greek and Roman," in *Encyclopedia of Religion and Ethics*, edited by James Hastings (New York: Charles Scribner's Sons, 1925), 12: 30.

10. Helen Silving, "Suicide and the Law," in *Clues to Suicide*, edited by Edwin S. Shneidman and Norman L. Farberow (New York: McGraw-Hill, 1957), 80–81.

11. A. Alverez, *The Savage God: A Study of Suicide* (New York: Bantam, 1976), 68.

12. Thomas Aquinas, *The "Summa Theologica" of Saint Thomas Aquinas*, vol. 10, edited by Fathers of the Dominican Province (London: Burns, Oates, and Washbourne, 1929), II, ii, Q.64, a.5: 202–5.

13. Thomas More, *Utopia*, translated by Paul Turner (New York: Penguin, 1981), 102.

14. Francis Bacon, *New Atlantis. A worke unfinished. Written by the Right Honourable Francis Lord Verulam, Viscount St. Alban* (London, 1629).

15. John Donne, *Complete Poetry and Selected Prose*, edited by John Hayward (London: Nonesuch Library), 195, 420–25, 783–84.

16. Jean-Jacques Rousseau, *The Social Contract and the Discourse on the Origins and Foundations of Inequality*, translated by G. D. H. Cole (New York: Knopf, 1993), 1712–78.

17. Tom L. Beauchamp and Seymur Perlin, *Ethical Issues in Death and Dying* (Englewood Cliffs: N.J.: Prentice-Hall, 1978), 105–21.

18. Emile Durkheim, *Suicide: A Study in Sociology*, edited by John A. Spalding and George Simpson (New York: Free Press, 1951).

19. David Stevenson, "Sigmund Freud: The Father of Psychoanalysis," Brown University, located at http://www.stg.brown.edu/projects/hypertext/landow/HTatBrown/freud/Biography.html in November 1997; and "Assisted Suicide," located at http://www.spectacle.org/295/sui.html in November 1997.

20. Humphry and Wickett, *The Right to Die*, 13–14.

21. *New York Times*, October 2, 1938.

22. *New York Times*, October 14, 1939.

23. Mildred Strunk, ed., "The Quarters Polls," *Public Opinion Quarterly* 11 (1947): 77.

24. Humphry and Wickett, *The Right to Die*, 36.

25. *New York Times*, April 23, 1939.

26. William Shirer, "Mercy Deaths in Germany," *Reader's Digest*, June 1941, 57.

27. Gerald Flemming, *Hitler and the Final Solution* (Berkeley: University of California Press, 1982), 20ff.

28. Humphry and Wickett, *The Right to Die*, 24–25.

29. Joseph Fletcher, "Our Right to Die," *Theology Today* 8 (1951): 202.

30. Ibid., 202–3.

31. "Attitudes of and towards the Dying," *Canadian Medical Association Journal* 87 (1962): 695.

32. O. Ruth Russell, *Freedom to Die* (New York: Human Sciences, 1977), 155.

33. Norman K. Brown, "The Preservation of Life," *Journal of the American Medical Association* 211 (1970): 76–83.

34. *New York Times*, August 2, 1973.

35. *Los Angeles Times*, April 3, 1975.

36. *In re Quinlan*, 137 N.J. Supr. 277 (Ch. Div. 1975).

37. "Guidelines for Discontinuance of Cardiopulmonary Life-Support Systems under Specified Circumstances" (adopted March 1981).

38. *Los Angeles Times*, January 1, 1985.

39. Melinda Lee, "Legalizing Assisted Suicide—Views of Physicians in Oregon," *New England Journal of Medicine* 334, (1996): 310–15.

40. Jerald Bachman, "Attitudes of Michigan Physicians and the Public toward Legalizing Physician-Assisted Suicide and Voluntary Euthanasia," *New England Journal of Medicine* 334, (1996): 303–9.

41. L. O. Gostin and R. F. Weir, "Life and Death Choices after Cruzan: Case Law and Reform on Medically Assisted Dying," *Journal of Law, Medicine, and Ethics* 21 (1993): 94–101.

42. Greg Pence, "Dr. Kevorkian and the Struggle for Physician-Assisted Suicide," *Bioethics* 9 (1995): 62–71.

43. Frank Murray, "Court Lets Assisted-Suicide Law Stand," *Washington Times*, October 15, 1997; Linda Greenhouse, "Assisted Suicide Clears a Hurdle in Highest Court," *New York Times*, October 15, 1997.

44. *Eugene Register-Guard*, April 24, 1997.

45. Todd Murphy, "Assisted-Suicide Law Survives in Oregon," *Yahoo News,* located at http://www.yahoo.cm/headlines/971105/news/stories/issues 2.html in November 1997.

46. Amy Goldstein, "No Drug Law Penalty for Assisted Suicides," *Washington Post*, June 6, 1998.

47. *New York Times*, October 2, 1996.

48. *Washington Post*, October 2, 1996.

Chapter 2: The Fundamental Issues

1. M. Batten, "Voluntary Euthanasia and the Risks of Abuse," *Law, Medicine, and Health Care* 20 (1992): 134; M. P. Batten, "Suicide: A Fundamental Human Right?" in *Suicide: The Philosophical Issues*, edited by M. P. Batten and D. J. Mayo (New York: St. Martin's Press, 1980), 267–85; D. Brock, "Voluntary Active Euthanasia," *Hastings Center Report* 22 (1992): 11; F. G. Miller and J. C. Flether, "The Case for Legalized Euthanasia," *Perspectives in Biology and Medicine* 36 (1993): 163–64.

2. Leonor Sampaio, "To Die with Dignity," *Social Science and Medicine* 35 (1992): 433–41; J. Rachels, *The End of Life* (New York: Oxford University Press, 1986), 181–82.

3. Brock, "Voluntary Active Euthanasia," 11.

4. 211 N.Y. 127, 129; 105 N.E. 92, 93 (1914).

5. *In re Yetter*, 62 Pa. D and C 2d 619 (1973); *Satz v. Perlmutter*, 362 S 2D 160 (Fla. App. 1978), affirmed by Florida Supreme Court 379 S 2D 359 (1980).

6. M. P. Batten, *The Least Worst Death* (Oxford: Oxford University Press, 1994), 102.

7. T. E. Quill and R. V. Brody, "'You Promised Me I Wouldn't Die Like This!' A Bad Death as a Medical Emergency," Archives of Internal Medicine 155 (1995): 1250–54.

8. G. A. Kasting, "The Nonnecessity of Euthanasia," in *Physician-Assisted Death*, edited by J. M. Humber, R. F. Almeder, and G. A. Kasting (Totowa, N.J.: Humana, 1993), 2545; R. F. Weir, "The Morality of Physician-Assisted Suicide," *Law, Medicine, and Health Care* 20 (1992): 123–24; Rachels, *The End of Life*, 152–54.

9. Voluntary Euthanasia Society, *The Last Right* (London: Voluntary Euthanasia Society, 1996).

10. T. L. Beauchamp and J. F. Childress, *Principles of Biomedical Ethics*, 3d ed. (New York: Oxford University Press, 1989), 227.

11. Daniel Callahan, "Can We Return Death to Disease?" *Hastings Center Report* 19 (1989): S5.

12. Leon Kass, "Neither for Love nor Money," *Public Interest* 94 (1989): 25–45.

13. E. J. Emanuel, "Euthanasia: Historical, Ethical, and Empiric Perspectives," *Archives of Internal Medicine* 154 (1994): 1890–1901; E. J. Emanuel, "The History of Euthanasia Debates in the United States and Britain," *Archives of Internal Medicine* 121 (1994): 793–802.

14. Elizabeth Markson, "To Be or Not to Be: Assisted Suicide Revisited," *Omega*, March 1995, 221–35; Harriet Tillock, "The Economy and Euthanasia or Assisted Elder Suicide," paper presented at the 1991 American Sociological Association Meeting.

15. M. P. Batten, "Manipulated Suicide," in *Suicide: The Philosophical Issues*, edited by M. P. Batten and D. J. Mayo (New York: St. Martins, 1980), 169–82.

16. Quoted in Nat Hentoff, "Class Warfare to the Death," *Village Voice*, July 1996, 12.

17. Damien Keown and John Keown, "Killing, Karma and Caring: Euthanasia in Buddhism and Christianity," *Journal of Medical Ethics* 21 (1995): 267.

18. H. Arkes et al., "Always to Care, Never to Kill," *First Things*, no. 18 (1992): 45–77.

19. A. Alverez, *The Savage God: A Study of Suicide* (New York: Bantam, 1976), 68.

20. Thomas Aquinas, *The "Summa Theologica" of Saint Thomas Aquinas*, vol. 10, edited by the Fathers of the Dominican Province (London: Burns, Oates, and Washbourne, 1929), II, ii, Q.64, a.5: 202–5.

21. Gerald Larue, *Euthanasia and Religion: A Survey of the Attitudes of World Religions to the Right to Die* (Los Angeles: Hemlock Society, 1985), 3.

22. Pope Pius XII 1958: 397.

23. Daniel Maguire, "A Catholic View of Mercy Killing," in *Beneficent Euthanasia*, edited by Marvin Kohl (Buffalo: Prometheus, 1975), 35.

24. W. R. Matthews, "Voluntary Euthanasia: The Ethical Aspect," in *Euthanasia and the Right to Die*, edited by A. B. Downing (London), 26.

25. Byron Sherwin, "Jewish Views of Euthanasia," in *Beneficent Euthanasia*, edited by Marvin Kohl (Buffalo: Prometheus, 1975), 7.

26. Immanuel Jakobovits, *Jewish Medical Ethics* (New York: Bloch, 1959), 121–25; "Euthanasia in Judaism," *Ha Pardes* 31, no. 1, 28–31, no. 3, 16–20; Charles Reines, "The Jewish Attitude toward Suicide," *Judaism* 10 (1961): 160–71; Solomon Freehof, *Reform Responsa Cincinnati* (Cincinnati: Hebrew Union College Press, 1960), 117–22.

27. *Semahoth* 1:1; Joseph Karo, *Shuhan Arukh, Yoreh Deah* 339:1; Moses Maimonides, "Laws of Mourning," *Mishneh Torah, Book of Judges*, 4:5.

28. Moshe Silberg, *Talmudic Law and the Modern State*, translated by Ben Zion Bokser (New York: Burning Bush, 1973), 68.

Chapter 3: Euthanasia in the United States and Canada

1. *Oregonian*, March 27, 1998.
2. *Philadelphia Inquirer*, May 28, 1998.

3. Robert Herty, *Death and the Right Hand* (Aberdeen: Cohen and West, 1960), 84–86.

4. Paul Starr, *The Social Transformation of American Medicine* (New York: Basic Books, 1982).

5. Abigail Trafford, "The Art of Dying, the Art of Living," *Washington Post*, July 1, 1997; C. K. Cassel and B. C. Vladeck, "ICD-9 Code for Palliative or Terminal Care," *New England Journal of Medicine* 335, (1996): 1232.

6. *Cruzan v. Director, Missouri Department of Health*, 497 U.S. 261 (1990).

7. "Twenty Years after Quinlan, New Cases Could Bolster the Right to Refuse Treatment," *Choices* 5 (1996): 1.

8. Mireya Navarro, "Assisted Suicide Decision Looms in Florida," *New York Times*, July 3, 1997.

9. "AIDS Patient Can Choose Suicide, Fla. Judge Rules," *Washington Post*, February 1, 1997.

10. "Florida Board Votes to Oppose Physician-Assisted Suicide," *Washington Post*, 10 February 1997.

11. Susan Cohen, "Old Glory," *Washington Post Magazine*, June 1, 1997.

12. Ibid.

13. "Vital Statistics," *Washington Post*, October 8, 1996.

14. Elaine Fox and Jeffrey Kamakahi, "Who's Fighting to Die? A Look at the Hemlock Society Membership," *Timelines*, July, August, September, 1996.

15. Shannon Brownlee and Joannie Schrof, "The Quality of Mercy," *U.S. News and World Report*, March 17, 1997.

16. Jan Hofmann, Neil Wenger, Roger Davis, Joan Teno, Alfred Connors Jr., Norman Desbiens, Joan Lynn, and Russell Phillips, "Patient Preferences for Communication with Physicians about End-of-Life Decisions," *Annals of Internal Medicine* 127 (1997): 1–12.

17. Charles Marwick, "Geriatricians Want Better End-of-Life Care," *Journal of the American Medical Association* 227 (12 February 1997): 445–46; Sheryl Gay Stolbert, "Cries of the Dying Awaken Doctors to a New Approach," *New York Times*, June 30, 1997.

18. Amy Goldstein, "Dying Patient's Care Varies Widely by Place, Study Says," *Washington Post*, October 15, 1997.

19. Cassel and Vladeck "ICD-9 Code for Palliative or Terminal Care."

20. Ira Byock, "Why Do We Make Dying So Miserable?" *Washington Post*, January 22, 1997.

21. "Why Hospice Is Not Always the Answer," *Hemlock Beacon Newsletter* (Spring 1997): 8.

22. Abigail Trafford, "World Health by the Numbers," *Washington Post*, June 3, 1997.

23. American Medical Association, Council on Ethical and Judicial Affairs, *Current Opinions of the Council on Ethical and Judicial Affairs* (Chicago: AMA, 1992).

24. Jerald Bachman, "Attitudes of Michigan Physicians and the Public toward Legalizing Physician-Assisted Suicide and Voluntary Euthanasia," *New England Journal of Medicine* 334 (1996): 303–9.

25. *USA Today*, April 12, 1996.

26. "Should Doctors Help Patients Die?" *Glamor*, May 1997, 199.

27. Diane Meier, "Doctors' Attitudes and Experiences with Physician-Assisted Death," in *Physician-Assisted Death*, edited by James M. Humber et al., (Totowa, N.J.: Humana, 1994).

28. Melinda Lee, "Legalizing Assisted Suicide—Views of Physicians in Oregon," *New England Journal of Medicine* 334 (1996): 310–15.

29. Jerald Bachman, "Attitudes of Michigan Physicians and the Public toward Legalizing Physician-Assisted Suicide and Voluntary Euthanasia."

30. Elizabeth Rosenthal, "When a Healer Is Asked, 'Help Me Die,' " *New York Times*, March 13, 1997.

31. Richard Knox, "Pleas for Death Are Studied; Requests, Fulfillments Seen about Equal in US, Netherlands," *Boston Globe*, March 27, 1996.

32. Raymond Leinbach, "Euthanasia Attitudes of Older Persons: A Cohort Analysis," *Research on Aging* 15 (1993): 443–48; Larry Seidlitz, Paul Duberstein, Christopher Cox, and Y. Conwell, "Attitudes of Older People toward Suicide and Assisted Suicide: An Analysis of Gallup Poll Findings," *Journal of American Geriatrics Society* 43 (1995): 993–98.

33. Anne Jordan, "Determinants of Attitudes toward Self-Selected and Mediated Death: Euthanasia, Suicide and Capital Punishment," paper presented at the 1995 American Sociological Association meeting.

34. David Rosenbaum, "Americans Want a Right to Die. Or So They Think," *New York Times*, June 8, 1997.

35. Don Colburn, "Many Seniors Would Seek Advice on Ending Life," *Washington Post*, May 13, 1997.

36. Joan Biskupic, "Supreme Court to Hear Physician-Assisted Suicide Cases Wednesday," *Washington Post*, January 5, 1997; Susan Okie, "Country's Doctors Remain Divided over Physician-Assisted Suicide," *Washington Post*, January 8, 1997.

37. Linda Greenhouse, "High Court to Say if the Dying Have a Right to Suicide Help," *New York Times*, October 2, 1996; *Washington v. Glucksberg*, 117 S. Ct. 2258 (1997), *Vacco v. Quill*, 117 S. Ct. 2293 (1997).

38. Joan Biskupic, "Court to Hear Two Cases on Right to Die," *Washington Post*, October 2, 1996.

39. Joan Biskupic, "Justices Skeptical of Assisted Suicide" *Washington Post*, January 9, 1997; Linda Greenhouse, "High Court Hears 2 Cases Involving Assisted Suicide," *New York Times,* January 9, 1997.

40. Joan Biskupic, "High Court Allows Bans on Assisted Suicide, Strikes down Law Restricting Online Speech—Decision Rejects 'Right' for Help in Killing Self," *Washington Post,* June 27, 1997; Janny Scott, "An Issue that Won't Die," *New York Times,* June 27, 1997.

41. F. Grunberg "Reflections on Assisted Suicide and Euthanasia," *Canadian Journal of Psychiatry* 40 (1995): 212–15; Russell Ogden, "The Right to Die: A Policy Proposal for Euthanasia and Aid in Dying," *Canadian Public Policy* 21 (1994): 1–25; Gene Stollerman, "Quality of Life: Treatment Decisions and the Third Alternative," *Journal of the American Geriatrics Society* 32 (1984): 483–84.

42. Karen Grant, "The Inverse Care Law in the Context of Universal Free Health Insurance in Canada: Toward Meeting Health Needs through Public Policy," *Sociological Focus* 17 (1984): 137–55; Elizabeth Rosenthal, "Canada's National Health Plan Gives Care to All, with Limits," *New York Times*, April 30, 1991; Eugene Vayda and Raisa Deber, "The Canadian Health Care System: An Overview," *Social Science and Medicine* 18 (1984): 191–97.

43. Wayne Kondro, "Will Canada Have 'Mercy Killing' Bill?" *Lancet* 345 (1995): 1562; The Special Senate Committee on Euthanasia and Assisted Suicide, *Of Life and Death—Final Report* (Ottowa, 1995), chaps. 3–7.

44. *Rodriguez v. A-G of British Columbia* (1993) 3 WWR 553; and Wayne Kondro, "Canada's Euthanasia Debate Renewed," *Lancet* 343 (1994): 534.

45. Howard Schneider, "Canada's 'Dr. Death' Issue—Murder Charge against Physician Puts New Focus on Ban on Assisted Suicide," *Washington Post,* July 15, 1997.

46. Graeme Hamilton, "Murder Case Dismissed—No Trial for Halifax Doctor; Some Senators Call for New Medical Laws," *Hamilton Spectator,* February 28, 1998, located at http://www.southam.com/hamiltonspectator/local/980228/1652876.html in May 1998.

47. Peter Singer, Sujit Choudhry, Jane Armstrong, Eric Meslin, and Frederick Lowy, "Public Opinion Regarding End-of-Life Decisions: Influences of Prognosis, Practice, and Process," *Social Science and Medicine* 41 (1995): 1517–21.

48. Dying with Dignity, Canada, and Gallup Canada Inc., "The Gallup Poll—Canadians Voice Their Opinions on Doctor-Assisted Suicide," located at http://www.web.apc.org/dwd/index.html in June 1997.

49. Charles Weijer, "Learning from the Dutch: Physician-Assisted Death, Slippery Slopes, and the Nazi Analogy," *Health Law Review* 4 (1995): 23–29.

Chapter 4: Euthanasia in the Netherlands, the United Kingdom, Germany, Switzerland, Spain, and France

1. G. Wal and R. Dillman, "Euthanasia in the Netherlands," *British Medical Journal* 308 (1994): 1346–49.

2. Helga Kushe, Peter Singer, Peter Blume, Malcolm Clark, and Maurice Rickard, "End-of-Life Decisions in Australian Medical Practice," *Medical Journal of Australia* 166 (1997): 191–96.

3. G. Kimsma and E. Leeuwen, "Dutch Euthanasia: Background, Practice, and Present Justifications," *Cambridge Quarterly of Healthcare Ethics* 2 (1993): 19–35.

4. Voluntary Euthanasia Society of Scotland (VESS), *Euthanasia in Holland, August 1996*, located at http://www.netlink.co.uk/users/vess/factaccs.html in September 1996.

5. A. Capron, "Euthanasia in the Netherlands: American Observations," *Hastings Center Report* 2, (1992): 30–33.

6. Leo Alexander, "Medical Science under Dictatorship," *New England Journal of Medicine* 241 (1949): 45.

7. *Time*, March 5, 1973, 70.

8. "To Cease upon the Midnight," *Economist*, September 17, 1994, 21–23; Carlos Gomez, *Regulating Death* (New York: Free Press, 1991).

9. J. Gevers, "Legal Developments Concerning Active Euthanasia on Request in the Netherlands," *Bioethics* 1 (1987): 156–62; Marcia Angell, "Euthanasia in the Netherlands," *New England Journal of Medicine* 335 (1996).

10. Chris Ciesielski-Carlucci and Gerrit Kimsma, "The Impact of Reporting Cases of Euthanasia in Holland: A Patient and Family Perspective," *Bioethics* 8 (1994): 151–58.

11. Roel Janssen, "The Euthanasia Question," *Europe* 339 (1994): 45; Voluntary Euthanasia Society, *The Last Right* (London: Voluntary Euthanasia Society, 1996).

12. Voluntary Euthanasia Society of Scotland, "Laws of Mourning," *Euthanasia in Holland*; Voluntary Euthanasia Society, *The Last Right.*

13. Voluntary Euthanasia Society of Scotland, *Euthanasia in Holland.*

14. H. Jochemsen, "Euthanasia in Holland: An Ethical Critique of the New Law," *Journal of Medical Ethics* 20 (1994): 212–17; Charles Weijer, "Learning from the Dutch: Physician-Assisted Death, Slippery Slopes, and the Nazi Analogy," *Health-Law Review* 4 (1995): 23–29; Voluntary Euthanasia Society of Scotland, *Euthanasia in Holland.*

15. Paul van der Maas, Gerrit van der Wal, Ilinka Haverkate, Carmen de Graaff, John Kester, Bregje Onwuteaka-Philipsen, Agnes van der Heide, Jacqueline Bosma, and Dick Willems, "Euthanasia, Physician-Assisted Suicide, and Other Medical Practices Involving the End of Life in the Netherlands, 1990–95," *New England Journal of Medicine* 335 (1996): 669–74 and 1699–1705; Gerrit van der Wal, Paul van der Maas, Jacqueline Bosma, Bregje Onwuteaka-Philipsen, Dick Willems, Ilinka Haverkate, and Piet Kostense, "Evaluation of the Notification Procedure for Physician-Assisited Death in the Netherlands," *New England Journal of Medicine* 335 (1996): 1706–11.

16. Roel Janssen, "The Euthanasia Question," *Europe,* no. 339 (1994): 45; S. Gevers, "Physician-Assisted Suicide in the Netherlands," *Bioethics* 9 (1995): 309–12.

17. "The Euthanasia War," *Economist*, June 21, 1997, 21–24.

18. "To Cease upon the Midnight."

19. Derek Humphry, "Swiss Surprise," *World Federation of Right-to-Die Societies Newsletter*, November 29, 1996, 1–2.

20. J. K. Mason and Deirdre Mulligan, "Euthanasia by Stages," *Lancet* 347, (1996): 810–11.

21. B. Dimond, "Filling in the Statutory Gas with the Common Law—An Analysis of the Mental Health Act 1983," *New Law Journal*, August 17, 1984, 693.

22. Sarah Ramsay, "UK Doctors Get Advance-Directive Guidance," *Lancet* 345 (1995): 913–14.

23. Mary Rose Barrington, "Euthanasia: An English Perspective," in *To Die or Not to Die? Cross-Disciplinary, Cultural, and Legal Perspectives on the Right to Choose Death*, edited by Arthur Berger and Joyce Berger (New York: Praeger, 1990).

24. S. G. Potts, "The Clinician versus the Crown," *Hastings Center Report* 23 (1993): 2–3.

25. Ross Kessel, "Euthanasia in Britain," *Hastings Center Report* 25 (1995): 51.

26. Chris Docker, "The Sanctity of Human Life and Personal Freedom," *Dying in Dignity, Mensa Sig News Journal* 2, located at http://www.euthanasia.org/didmsnj.html in July 1996.

27. Martin Wall, "Irish Supreme Court Approves 'Right-to-Die' Case," *Lancet* 346 (1995): 368.

28. Diana Brahams, "Parents Seek Right to Allow Boy in UK to Die," *Lancet* 346 (1995): 368.

29. Stephen White, "Mercy Killer Is Set Free; Brother Begged to Die; Court Frees Mercy Killing Brother," *Daily Mirror,* October 15, 1996; Tony Wallin, "Mercy Killer Walks Free," *Scottish Daily Record*, October 15, 1996.

30. Rebecca English, "Put My Cancer Son's Hired Killers in Jail," *Express*, August 6, 1997.

31. Clare Dyer, "Two Doctors Confess to Helping Patients to Die," *British Medical Journal* 315 (1997): 1332–34.

32. Rory Williams, "Awareness and Control of Dying: Some Paradoxical Trends in Public Opinion," *Sociology of Health and Illness* 11 (1989): 201–12.

33. Voluntary Euthanasia Society, *The Last Right.*

34. Jacqui Wise, "Public Supports Euthanasia for Most Desperate Cases," *British Medical Journal* 313 (1996), located at http://www.bmj.com/bmj/archive/curr.htm in December 1996; David Donnison and Caroline Bryson, "Matters of Life and Death: Attitudes to Euthanasia," in *British Social Attitudes, 1996–1997*, edited by Roger Jowell, John Curtice, Alison Park, Lindsay Brook, and Katarina Thompson (Aldershot: Dartmouth Publishing, 1996), chap. 8.

35. Sheila McLean and Alison Britton, *Sometimes a Small Victory* (Glasgow: Glasgow University Institute of Law and Ethics in Medicine, 1996).

36. Karen Birchard, "Many Irish Doctors in Favor of Physician-Assisted Suicide," *Lancet* 350 (1997), located at http://www.thelancet.com/lancet/User/vol350no9079/news/index.html#manyirish.

37. Margaret Pabst Batten, *The Least Worst Death: Essays in Bioethics on the End of Life*,(New York: Oxford University Press, 1994), 254–70.

38. Volker Krey, "Ttung durch Zulassen eines Selbstmordes" (Killing by Allowing a Suicide to Occur), *Strafrecjt Bespmderer Teil*, 7th ed. (Stuttgart: Verlag W. Kohlhammer, 1989): 35–37.

39. "To Cease upon the Midnight."

40. W. Deuel, *People under Hitler* (New York: Harcourt, Brace, 1942).

41. Michael Burleigh, "Racism as Social Policy: The Nazi Euthanasia Programme," *Ethnic and Racial Studies* 14 (1991): 453–73.

42. Michael Burleigh, "Psychiatry, German Society, and the Nazi Euthanasia Programme," *Social History of Medicine* 7 (1994): 213–28.

43. Benoit Massin and Pierre Thuillier, "Nazism and Science," *Recherche* 21 (1990): 1562–75.

44. Joachim Hohmann, "National Socialist 'Euthanasia' in Saxon Institutions and Its Penal Law Punishment in the Soviet Occupied Zone," *Historical Social Research* 20 (1995): 31–60.

45. Wertham. *The German Euthanasia Program* (Cincinnati: Hayes, 1977).

46. Tricare Europe, "Country Profile: Germany," *Regional Health Services Plan (RHSP)*, Section 12.1 (1997), located at http://webserver.europe.tricare.-osd.mil/main/rhsp/germany2.html in September 1997.

47. Batten, *The Least Worst Death*, 254–70.

48. Derek Humphry, *The Right to Die: Understanding Euthanasia* (New York: Harper and Row, 1986), 221.

49. Humphry, "Swiss Surprise," 1.

50. Jeanne Marchig, president of EXIT A.D.M.D. Suisse romande, letter to author, November 8, 1996.

51. Ramon Sanpedro & Running on Empty, interview conducted by Chris Docker for DeathNet, located at http://www.islandnet.com/~deathnet/sanpedro.html in September 1997.

52. Voluntary Euthanasia Society, "Spanish Initiative," *VES Newsletter* 61 (1997), located at http://dialspace.dial.pipex.com/ves.london/newslet/world.htm in September 1997.

53. Embassy of Spain, "The National Health Institute: Insalud," located at http://www.sispain.org/SiSpain/english/health/institut.html in September 1997.

54. Tricare Europe, "Country Profile: Spain," *Regional Health Services Plan*, located at http://webserver.europe.tricare.osd.mil/main/rhsp/spain3.html in September 1997.

Chapter 5: Euthanasia in Australia, China, Japan, and India

1. "Darwinian Death," *Economist*, February 18, 1995, 34; Gerald Stewart, "Australia's Euthanasia Legislation Runs into Difficulties," *Deutsche Presse-Agentur*, July 12,1996.

2. David Nason, " 'Dent Was a Man of Courage': Perron," *Australian*, September 26, 1996.

3. Northern Territory of Australia Rights of the Terminally Ill Act, 1996, and Rights of the Terminally Ill, Amendment Act, 1996.

4. Kevin Andrews, "It's a National Responsibility to Invalidate Lethal Injections," *Australian*, September 26, 1996; Ewin Hannan and David Nason, "Kennett Attacks 'Immoral' Attempt to Override NT Law," *Australian*, September 26, 1996; Belinda Hickman, Katherine Glascott, and Jody Scott, "Ethical Dilemma: Churches Unite in Condemnation," *Australian*, September 26, 1996; "Plea from Australian Who Took his own Life Legally," *Deutsche Presse-Agentur*, September 26, 1996.

5. Nason, " 'Dent was a Man of Courage': Perron"; Nicholas Rothwell, "My Father Decided to Die in Dignity," *Australian*, September 26, 1996.

6. Hickman, Glascott, and Scott, "Ethical Dilemma."

7. Mark Dowdney, "Dr. Death Claims a Willing Victim: Cancer Victim Bob Dent Has Become the First Person to Commit Legally-Assisted Suicide, It

Was Revealed Yesterday," *Scottish Daily Record & Sunday Mail Ltd.*, September 27, 1996.

8. Katherine Glascott, "Push the Button and Die Peacefully," *Australian*, September 26, 1996.

9. Robert Dent, "Why I Chose to Die," *Australian*, September 26, 1996.

10. Kerry-Anne Walsh, "Vote . . . Life, Death, Choice. Will to Die: Australians Expect the Freedom to Manage Their Lives—So Why Not Their Deaths?" *Bulletin*, September 17, 1996.

11. Helga Kuhse and Peter Singer, "Doctors' Practices and Attitudes Regarding Voluntary Euthanasia," *Medical Journal of Australia* 148 (1988): 623–27.

12. Helga Kuhse and Peter Singer, "Euthanasia: A Survey of Nurses' Attitudes and Practices," *Australian Nurses' Journal* 21 (1992).

13. Peter Blume and Emma O'Malley, "Euthanasia: Attitudes and Practices of Medical Practitioners," *Medical Journal of Australia* 181 (1994): 137.

14. Helga Kuhse, Peter Singer, Peter Blume, Malcolm Clark, and Maurice Rickard, "End-of-Life Decisions in Australian Medical Practice," *Medical Journal of Australia* 166 (1997): 191–96.

15. Janet Fife-Yeomans, "Patients Face a Legal Minefield across the Nation," *Australian*, September 26, 1996; "The Law State by State," *Australian*, September 26, 1996.

16. Walsh, "Vote . . . Life, Death, Choice."

17. Fife-Yeomans, "Patients Face a Legal Minefield across the Nation"; "First Legal Death Splits the Nation," *Australian*, September 26, 1996.

18. Gabrielle Chan, "Bill Won't Punish Doctors Involved in Euthanasia," *Australian*, September 26, 1996.

19. Voluntary Euthanasia Society of Victoria, "77% of Voters in Kevin Andrews's Electorate Opposed to Anti-Euthanasia Bill," media release, March 12, 1997, located at http://pi.taunet.net.au/deliverance/current.htm in April 1997.

20. Karen Middleton, "Harsh Language in Death Bill Debate," *Age,* March 19, 1997.

21. Alan Thornhill, "Australia Repeals Euthanasia Law," *Washington Post*, March 25, 1997.

22. Sian Watkins, "States Urged to Pass Their Own Laws," *Age*, March 26, 1997.

23. S. Karene Witcher, "Northern Territory, a Place Apart, Learns Price of Euthanasia," *Wall Street Journal*, January 22, 1997; Melissa Fyfe, "Doctor Feeling the Strain of Fame," *Age*, October 17, 1996.

24. "First Legal Death Splits the Nation."

25. Gerald Stewart, "Australia's Euthanasia Legislation Runs into Difficulties," *Deutche Presse-Agentur* July 12, 1996.

26. Hickman, Glascott, and Scott, "Ethical Dilemma."

27. South Australia Voluntary Euthanasia Society, *Did You Know? Public Opinion*, SAVES Fact Sheet No. 2, located at http://easyweb.easynet.co.uk/~didmsnj/saves/safs.htm in August 1996.

28. Kuhse et al., "End-of Life Decisions in Australian Medical Practice."

29. Vera Rich, "Will the Chinese Legalise Euthanasia?" *Lancet* 345 (1995): 783.

30. Ibid.

31. "To Cease upon the Midnight," *Economist*, September 17, 1994, 21–23.

32. A. Herxheimer, "Euthanasia and Palliative Care: A Psueduconflict?" *Lancet* 348 (1996): 1187.

33. Howard Brody, "Bioethics in Japan: At First Glance," *Medical Humanities Report* 18 (1997), located at http://www.chm.msu.edu/centerethicshumanities/mhr/w97japan.html.

34. Shigeru Kato, "Japanese Perspectives on Euthanasia," in *To Die or Not to Die? Cross-Disciplinary, Cultural, and Legal Perspectives on the Right to Choose Death*, edited by Arthur Berger and Joyce Berger (New York: Praeger, 1990).

35. Herxheimer, "Euthanasia and Palliative Care."

36. "Kyoto 'Mercy Killing' Not Rare in Japan, Doctor Says," Kyodo News International, *Japan Policy & Politics*, June 24, 1996.

37. "Half of Doctors Get Requests Not to Prolong Life," *Japan Economic Newswire*, July 2, 1996.

38. "Newspaper Poll Shows Majority Allowing Euthanasia," *Japan Economic Newswire*, October 2, 1996.

39. Ezra Vogel, *Japan as Number One: Lessons for America* (Cambridge: Harvard University Press, 1979).

40. United Nations Development Program, *Human Development Report* (New York: Oxford University Press, 1993); World Bank, *World Development Report* (Washington, D.C.: World Bank, 1993).

41. H. Fedden, *Suicide: A Social and Historical Study* (New York: Benjamin Blom, 1972), 25.

42. Daya Shanker, "Indian Legal Concepts of the Right to Die," in *To Die or Not to Die? Cross-Disciplinary, Cultural, and Legal Perspectives on the Right to Choose Death*, edited by Arthur Berger and Joyce Berger (New York: Praeger, 1990).

43. Robert Barry, *Breaking the Thread of Life on Rational Suicide* (New Brunswick: Transaction, 1994), 61–64.

44. J. Jagmanderlal, *Outlines of Jainism* (Cambridge: Cambridge University Press, 1940), 69.

45. N. Smart, *The World's Religions* (Englewood Cliffs, N.J.: Prentice-Hall, 1989), 68.

46. United Nations Development Program, *Human Development Report*; World Bank, *World Development Report*.

Chapter 6: Euthanasia in Colombia, South Africa, Iran, and Israel

1. Fundacion Pro Derecho A Morir Dignamente, *Reflexiones en Torno del Derecho a Morir Dignamente, La Eutanasia* (Bogota: Fundacion Pro Derecho A Morir Dignamente).

2. Pan American Health Organization, "Country Health Profiles, Colom-

bia," located at http://www.paho.org/english/colombia.html in September 1997.

3. Tim Johnson, "Legal Euthanasia Unsettles Colombia," *Miami Herald*, June 30, 1997, located at http://www.herald.com in July 1997.

4. Serge Kovaleski, "Colombia Debates Court Ruling that Legalizes Mercy Killing," *Washington Post*, August 18, 1997.

5. Jerold Leonard-Taitz, "Euthanasia, Human Rights, and the Law," *SAVES Newsletter—The Living Will Society* 28 (1992): 2.

6. "Legal Aspects," *SAVES Newsletter—The Living Will Society* 29 (1993): 1.

7. "What Are We Waiting For?" *SAVES Newsletter—The Living Will Society* 32 (1996): 1.

8. South African Law Commission, *Euthanasia and the Artificial Preservation of Life*, Johannesburg Discussion Paper 71 Project 86, June 30, 1997, 12.

9. Ibid.

10. Ibid.

11. Jalaluddin Umri, "Suicide or Termination of Life," translated by S. A. H. Rizvi, *Islam and Comparative Law Quarterly* 7 (1987): 136–44.

12. Vardit Rispler-Chaim, *Islamic Medical Ethics in the Twentieth Century* (New York: E. J. Brill, 1993), 94–99.

13. M. Adil As Aseer, "An Islamic Perspective on Terminating Life-Sustaining Measures," in *To Die or Not to Die? Cross-Disciplinary, Cultural, and Legal Perspectives on the Right to Choose Death*, edited by Arthur Berger and Joyce Berger (New York: Praeger, 1990), 59–65.

14. Byron Sherwin, "Jewish Views of Euthanasia," in *Beneficent Euthanasia,* edited by Marvin Kohl (Buffalo: Prometheus, 1975), 7.

15. Fred Rosner, "Risks versus Benefits in Treating the Gravely Ill Patient: Ethical and Religious Considerations," in *Jewish Values in Bioethics*, edited by Rabbi Levi Meier (New York: Human Sciences, 1986).

16. Zev Schostak, "Jewish Ethical Guidelines for Resuscitation and Artificial Nutrition and Hydration of the Dying Elderly," *Journal of Medical Ethics*, no. 2 (1994): 93–100.

17. Israel Society for the Right to Die with Dignity, *General Information Document* (Israel Society for the Right to Die with Dignity, 1996).

18. Jeremy Maissel, "Euthanasia: Who Plays God?" *Jerusalem Post*, January 4, 1997.

19. Immanuel Jakobovits, *Jewish Medical Ethics* (New York: Bloch 1959), 121–25; "Euthanasia in Judaism," *Ha Pardes* 31, no. 1, 28–31, 16–20; Charles Reines, "The Jewish Attitude toward Suicide," *Judaism* 10 (1961): 160–71; Solomon Freehof, *Reform Responsa* (Cincinnati: Hebrew Union College Press, 1960), 117–22.

20. *Semahoth* 1:1; Joseph Karo, *Shulan Arukh, Yoreh Deah* 339:1; Moses Maimonides,"Laws of Mourning," *Mishneh Torah, Book of Judges,* 4:5.

21. Moshe Silberg, *Talmudic Law and the Modern State*, translated by Ben Zion Bokser (New York: Burning Bush, 1973), 68.

22. Immanuel Jakobovits, "Ethical Problems Regarding the Termination of

Life," in *Jewish Values in Bioethics*, edited by Rabbi Levi Meier (New York: Human Sciences, 1986.

Chapter 7: Toward a Workable Social Policy

1. Mildred Strunk,"The Quarters Polls," *Public Opinion Quarterly* 11 (1947): 77.

2. *New York Times*, April 23, 1939.

3. American Medical Association, Council on Ethical and Judicial Affairs, *Current Opinions of the Council on Ethical and Judicial Affairs* (Chicago: AMA, 1992).

4. Jerald Bachman, "Attitudes of Michigan Physicians and the Public toward Legalizing Physician-Assisted Suicide and Voluntary Euthanasia," *New England Journal of Medicine* 334 (1996): 303–9.

5. "Should Doctors Help Patients Die?" *Glamor*, May 1997, 199.

6. Jacqui Wise, "Public Supports Euthanasia for Most Desperate Cases," *British Medical Journal* 313 (1996); David Donnison and Caroline Bryson, "Matters of Life and Death: Attitudes to Euthanasia," *British Social Attitudes 1996–1997*, edited by Roger Jowell, John Curtice, Alison Park, Lindsay Brook, and Katarina Thompson (Dartmouth Publishing, 1996).

7. Sheila McLean and Alison Britton, *Sometimes a Small Victory* (Glasgow: Glasgow University, Institute of Law and Ethics in Medicine, 1996).

8. Peter Singer, Sujit Choudhry, Jane Armstrong, Eric Meslin, and Frederick Lowry, "Public Opinion Regarding End-of-Life Decisions: Influences of Prognosis, Practice and Process," *Social Science and Medicine* 41 (1995): 1517–21.

9. Dying with Dignity, Canada, and Gallup Canada Inc., "The Gallup Poll—Canadians Voice Their Opinions on Doctor-Assisted Suicide," located at http://www.web.apc.org/dwd/index.html in June 1997.

10. Vera Rich, "Will the Chinese Legalise Euthanasia?" *Lancet* 345 (1995): 783.

11. Kerry-Anne Walsh, "Vote . . . Life, Death, Choice. Will to Die: Australians Expect the Freedom to Manage Their Lives—So Why Not Their Deaths?" *Bulletin*, September 17, 1996.

12. Voluntary Euthanasia Society of Victoria, "77% of Voters in Kevin Andrews's Electorate Opposed to Anti-Euthanasia Bill," media release, March 12, 1997, located at http://pi.taunet.net.an/deliverance/current.htm in April 1997.

13. O. Ruth Russell, *Freedom to Die* (New York: Human Sciences, 1977).

14. Diane Meier, "Doctors' Attitudes and Experiences with Physician-Assisted Death," in *Physician-Assisted Death*, edited by James M. Humber et al. (Totowa, N.J.: Humana, 1994).

15. Melinda Lee, "Legalizing Assisted Suicide—Views of Physicians in Oregon," *New England Journal of Medicine* 334 (1996): 310–15.

16. Jerald Bachman, "Attitudes of Michigan Physicians and the Public toward Legalizing Physician-Assisted Suicide and Voluntary Euthanasia," *New England Journal of Medicine* 334 (1996): 303–9.

17. Richard Knox, "Pleas for Death Are Studied; Requests, Fulfillments Seen about Equal in US, Netherlands," *Boston Globe*, March 27, 1996.

18. Karen Birchard, "Many Irish Doctors in Favor of Physician-Assisted Suicide," *Lancet* 350 (1997), located at http://www.thelancet.com/lancet/user/vol350no9079/news/index/html#manyirish.

19. Helen Kuhse and Peter Singer, "Doctors' Practices and Attitudes Regarding Voluntary Euthanasia," *The Medical Journal of Australia* 148 (1988): 623–27.

20. "Half of Doctors get Requests Not to Prolong Life," *Japan Economic Newswire*, July 2, 1996.

21. *The Washington Post*, June 6, 1998.

22. Charles Stannard, "Old Folks and Dirty Work: The Social Conditions for Patient Abuse in a Nursing Home," in *Aging, the Individual and Society: Readings in Social Gerontology*, edited by Jill Quadagno (New York: St. Martin's, 1980), 501.

23. James Rachels, *The End of Life—Euthanasia and Morality* (Oxford: Oxford University Press, 1986), 49–50.

Suggested Reading

American Academy of Hospice and Palliative Medicine. "Comprehensive End-of-Life Care and Physician-Assisted Suicide." Located at http://www.aahpm.org/pas.htm in May 1998.

American Medical Association, Council on Ethical and Judicial Affairs. *Current Opinions of the Council on Ethical and Judicial Affairs.* Chicago: AMA, 1992.

Andrews, Kevin. "It's a National Responsibility to Invalidate Lethal Injections." *Australian*, September 26, 1996.

Annas, George. "The Bell Tolls for a Constitutional Right to Physician-Assisted Suicide." *New England Journal of Medicine* 337 (1997): 1098.

Bachman, Jerald. "Attitudes of Michigan Physicians and the Public toward Legalizing Physician-Assisted Suicide and Voluntary Euthanasia." *New England Journal of Medicine* 334 (1996): 303–9.

Bagnall, Diana. "Last Rights, Final Question." *Bulletin*, September 17, 1996.

Bates, Erica. "Decision Making in Critical Illness." *Australian and New Zealand Journal of Sociology* 15 (1979): 45–54.

Bernhoft, Robin. "How We Can Win the Compassion Debate." *Citizen Magazine*, June 24, 1996. Located at http://www.aapainmanage.org/aapm/art/art1.htm in May 1998.

Biskupic, Joan. "Court to Hear Two Cases of Right-to-Die." *Washington Post*, October 2, 1996.

———. "Unanimous Decision Points to Tradition of Valuing Life." *Washington Post*, June 27, 1997.

Black, Albert. "Jonestown—Two Faces of Suicide: A Durkheimian Analysis." *Suicide and Life Threatening Behavior* 20 (1990): 285–304.

Breshnahan, James. "Palliative Care or Assisted Suicide?" *America* 178 (1998): 16–21.

Brody, H., and Gregg Vandekief. "Physician-Assisted Suicide: A Very Personal Issue." *American Family Physician* 55 (1997). Located at http:www.aafp.org/afp/970515ap/editoria.html in May 1998.

Burleigh, Michael. "Psychiatry, German Society, and the Nazi Euthanasia Programme." *Social History of Medicine* 7 (1994): 213–28.

———. "Racism as Social Policy: The Nazi Euthanasia Programme." *Ethnic and Racial Studies* 14 (1991): 453–73.

Ceresa, Maria. "Final Hours of a Five-Year Struggle." *Australian*, September 26, 1996.

Chan, Gabrielle. "Bill Won't Punish Doctors Involved in Euthanasia." *Australian*, September 26, 1996.

Choices in Dying. *Choices, the Newsletter of Choice in Dying: In the Legislatures & Courts*. New York: Choices in Dying, 1996.

Clouser, K. "The Challenge for Future Debate on Euthanasia." *Journal of Pain and Symptom Management* 6 (1991): 306–11.

"Colombia's Legalized Euthanasia Decried." *Philadelphia Inquirer*. Located at http://www.phillynews.com/inquirer/97/Oct/05/international/EUTH05.htm in October 1997.

"Court Unanimously Rules against Doctor-Asissted Suicide." *USA Today*, June 26, 1997. Located at http://www.usatoday.com/news/court/nscot645.htm in May 1998.

"Darwinian Death." *Economist*, February 18, 1995, 34.

Dent, Robert. "Why I Chose to Die." *Australian*, September 26, 1996.

Deuel, W. *People under Hitler.* New York: Harcourt, Brace, 1942.

Egan, Timothy. "First Death under an Assisted-Suicide Law." *New York Times,* March 26, 1998.

Eure, Rob. "Some Expected Other States to Follow Oregon; the First Two Suicides of the Death with Dignity Act Are Expected to Help Advocates Seeking Similar Meatures Elsewhere." *Oregonian*, March 27, 1998. Located at http://www.oregonian.com/todaysnews/9803/st03273.html in May 1998.

"Euthanasia and the Artificial Preservation of Life." Discussion Document 71. June 1997. Located at http://www.healthlink.org.za/pphc/phila/euthanas.htm in May 1998.

"Fewer Oncologists Support Assisted Suicide." *Yahoo News Health Headlines.* Located at http://dailynews.yahoo.com/headlin . . . /980519/health/stores/doc3_1.html in May 1998.

Fife-Yeomans, Jannet. "Patients Face a Legal Minefield across the Nation." *Australian*, September 26, 1996.

"First Legal Death Splits the Nations." *Australian*, September 26, 1996.

Fundacion Pro Derecho A Morir Dignamente. *Reflexiones en Torno del Derecho a Morir Dignamente. La Eutanasia*. Bogota: Fundacion Pro Derecho A Morir Dignamente.

Gallup, Inc. *Dying with Dignity.* 1996. Located at http://www.web.apc.org/dwd/index.html.

Gevers, J. "Legal Developments Concerning Active Euthanasia on Request in the Netherlands." *Bioethics* 1 (1987): 156–62.

Gevers, Sjef. "Physician-Assisted Suicide: New Developments in the Netherlands." *Bioethics* 9 (1995): 309–12.

Glascott, Katherine. "Push the Button and Die Peacefully." *Australian*, September 26, 1996.

Goldstein, Amy. "No Drug Law Penalty for Assisted Suicides." *Washington Post*, June 6, 1998.

Glushkov, V. "Sociological and Legal Questions of Euthanasia." *Sotsiologicheskie-Issledovaniya* 19 (1992): 12–19.

Gomez, Carlos. *Regulating Death.* New York: Free Press, 1991.

Gostin, L. O., and R. F. Weir. "Life and Death Choices after Cruzan: Case Law and Reform on Medically Assisted Dying." *Journal of Law, Medicine & Ethics* 21 (1993): 94–101.

Greenhouse, Linda. "Assisted Suicide Clears Challenge in Supreme Court; Oregon Law up to Voters." *New York Times*, October 15, 1997.

———. "High Court to Say if the Dying Have a Right to Suicide Help." *New York Times*, October 2, 1996.

Grunberg, F. "Reflections on Assisted Suicide and Euthanasia." *Canadian Journal of Psychiatry* 40 (1995): 212–15.

Hannan, Ewin, and David Nason. "Kennett Attacks 'Immoral' Attempt to Override NT Law." *Australian*, September 26, 1996.

Hemlock Society. *Physician Assistance in Dying: Update on Legislative Action by State*. Denver: Hemlock Society, 1996.

Hentoff, Nat. "Class Warfare to the Death." *Village Voice*, July 1996, 12.

Hickman, Belinda, Katherine Glascott, and Jody Scott. "Ethical Dilemma: Churches Unite in Condemnation." *Australian*, September 26, 1996.

Hoefler, James M. *Managing Death.* Boulder, Colo.: Westview, 1997.

Hoover, Erin, and Gail Kinsey Hill. "Two Die Using Suicide Law." *Oregonian*, March 26, 1998. Located at wysiwyg://86/http://www.oregonian.com/todaysnews/9803/st03261.html in May 1998.

Humphry, Derek. *The Right to Die: Understanding Euthanasia.* New York: Harper and Row, 1986.

———. *World Federation of Right-to-Die Societies Newsletter*, November 29, 1996.

Janssen, Roel. "The Euthanasia Question." *Europe* 339 (1994): 45.

Jecker, Nancy. "Physician-Assisted Death in the Netherlands and the United States: Ethical and Cultural Aspects of Health Policy Development." *Journal of the American Geriatrics Society* 42 (1994): 6672–78.

Jochemsen, H. "Euthanasia in Holland: An Ethical Critique of the New Law." *Journal of Medical Ethics* 20 (1994): 212–17.

Jordan, Anne. "Determinants of Attitudes toward Self-Selected and Mediated Death: Euthanasia, Suicide, and Capital Punishment." Paper presented at the 1995 American Sociological Association meeting.

Kamisar, Yale. "Are Laws against Assisted Suicide Constitutional?" Hastings Center Report 23 (1993): 32–41.

Kass, Leon. "Neither for Love nor Money." *Public Interest* 94 (1989): 25–45.

Keown, Damien, and John Keown. "Killing, Karma, and Caring: Euthanasia in Buddhism and Christianity." *Journal of Medical Ethics* 21 (1995): 265–69.

"The Law State by State." *Australian*, September 26, 1996.

Lee, Melinda. "Legalizing Assisted Suicide: Views of Physicians in Oregon." *New England Journal of Medicine* 334 (1996): 310–15.

Leinbach, Raymond. "Euthanasia Attitudes of Older Persons: A Cohort Analysis." *Research on Aging* 15 (1993): 433–48.

Loconte, Joe. "Hospice, not Hemlock: The Medical and Moral Rebuke to Doctor-Assisted Suicide." *Policy Review*, no. 88 (1998): 40–48.

"MD's Lawyer Hopes for 'Mercy-Killing' Law." *DeathNet*, June 12, 1997. Located at http://www.rights.org/deathnet/Cnews_9706.html in May 1998.

Markson, Elizabeth. "To Be or Not to Be: Assisted Suicide Revisited." *Omega*, March 1995, 221–35.

Massin, Benoit, and Pierre Thuillier. "Nazism and Science." *Recherche* 21 (1990): 1562–75.

McCormick, Richard. "Vive la Difference! Killing and Allowing to Die." *America* 177 (1997): 6–12.

Meier, Diane. *Doctors' Attitudes and Experiences with Physician-Assisted Death.* In *Physician-Assisted Death*, edited by James M. Humber et al. Totowa, N.J.: Humana, 1994.

Miller, F. G., and H. Brody. "Professional Integrity and Physician-Assisted Death." *Hastings Center Report* 25 (1995): 8–17.

Nason, David. " 'Dent Was a Man of Courage': Perron." *Australian*, September 26, 1996.

"News-In-Brief." *British Medical Journal* 316 (1998). Located at http://194.216.217.166/reg/archive/71347/7134n16.htm in May 1998.

"Northern Territory Euthanasia Law under Threat." *Japan Economic Newswire*, October 29, 1996.

Novakovic, D. "Euthanasia and Situations of Dying." *Revija-za-Sociologiju* 21 (1990): 193–252.

Ogden, Russell. "The Right to Die: A Policy Proposal for Euthanasia and Aid in Dying." *Canadian Public Policy* 21 (1994): 1–25.

"Oregon Escalates Its Heated Right-to-Die Debate." *Christian Science Monitor*, April 8, 1998.

Pence, Greg. "Dr. Kevorkian and the Struggle for Physician-Assisted Suicide." *Bioethics* 9 (1995): 62–71.

In re Quinlan, 70 N.J. 10, 355 A.2d 647, 665, 670 and fn 9 (1976).

Ramsay, Sarah. "UK Doctors Get Advance-Directive Guidance." *Lancet*, April 8, 1995, 913–14.

"Report: Change Canada's Criminal Code." *Yahoo News Health Headlines*, August 13, 1997. Located at http://biz.yahoo.com/upi/97/08/13/international_news/canadahos_1.html in May 1998.

Rosenbaum, David. "Americans Want a Right to Die. Or So They Think." *New York Times*, June 8, 1997.

Rothwell, Nicholas. "My Father Decided to Die in Dignity." *Australian*, September 26, 1996.

Sampaio, Leonor. "To Die with Dignity." *Social Science and Medicine* 35 (1992): 433–41.

Schostak, Zev. "Jewish Ethical Guidelines for Resuscitation and Artificial Nutrition and Hydration of the Dying Elderly." *Journal of Medical Ethics* 21 (1994): 93–100.

Seidlitz, Larry, Paul Duberstein, Christopher Cox, and Y. Conwell. "Attitudes of Older People toward Suicide and Assisted Suicide: An Analysis of Gallup Poll Findings." *Journal of American Geriatrics Society* 43 (1995): 993–98.

Shapiro, Joseph. "On Second Thought: Oregon Reconsiders Its Pioneering Assisted-Suicide Law." *US News & World Report*, September 1, 1997, 58.

Singer, Peter, Sujit Choudhry, Jane Armstrong, Eric Meslin, and Frederick Lowy. "Public Opinion Regarding End-of-Life Decisions: Influences Prognosis, Practice, and Process." *Social Science and Medicine* 41 (1995): 1517–21.

South Australian Voluntary Euthanasia Society (SAVES). *Voluntary Euthanasia in the Netherlands*. Fact Sheet no. 4. August 1996. Located at http://easyweb-.easynet.co.uk/~didmsnj/saves/safs.htm.

Spurgeon, David. "Canadian Doctor Charged with Murder." *British Medical Journal* 314 (1997). Located at http://194.216.217.166/reg/archive/7095n11.htm in May 1998.

"State of the Catholic Health Association." *Fatima Network News*, November 5, 1998. Located at http://www.fatima.org/suicide/html in May 1998.

Stolberg, Sheryl. "Considering the Unthinkable: Protocol for Assisted Suicide." *New York Times*, June 11, 1997.

———. "In Death, the Goal Is No Questions Asked." *New York Times*, April 26, 1998.

Stollerman, Gene. "Quality of Life: Treatment Decisions and the Third Alternative." *Journal of the American Geriatrics Society* 32 (1984): 483–84.

Tillock, Harriet. "The Economy and Euthanasia or Assisted Elder Suicide." Paper presented at the 1991 American Sociological Association meeting.

"To Cease upon the Midnight." *Economist*, September 17, 1994, 21–23.

Townsend, Liz. "Colombia's Highest Court Legalizes Euthanasia." *National Right to Life News*. Located at http://www.euthanasia.com/colum2.html in May 1998.

Van der Maas, Paul, Gerrit van der Wal, Ilinka Haverkate, Carmen de Graaff, John Kester, Bregje Onwuteaka-Philipsen, Agnes van der Heide, Jacqueline Bosma, and Dick Willems. "Euthanasia, Physician-Assisted Suicide, and Other Medical Practices Involving the End of Life in the Netherlands, 1990–1995." *New England Journal of Medicine* 335 (1996): 1699–1705.

Van der Wal, Gerrit, Paul van der Maas, Jacqueline Bosma, Bregje Onwuteaka-Philipsen, Dick Willems, Ilinka Haverkate, Piet Kostense. "Evaluation of the Notification Procedure for Physician-Assisted Death in the Netherlands." *New England Journal of Medicine* 335 (1996): 1706–11.

Voluntary Euthanasia Society. *The Last Right*. London: Voluntary Euthanasia Society, 1996.

Voluntary Euthanasia Society of London. "World Summary." Located at http://dspace.dial.pipex.com/ves.london/world.htm in May 1998.

Voluntary Euthanasia Society of Scotland. *Euthanasia and Assisted Suicide around the World*. April 1998. Located at http://www.netlink.co.uk/users/vess/else.html in May 1998.

———. *Euthanasia in Holland*. August 1996. Located at http://www.netlink.-co.uk/users/vess/factaccs.html.

Wall, Martin. "Irish Supreme Court Approves 'Right-To-Die' Case," *Lancet*, August 5, 1995, 368.

Walsh, Edward. "Split Verdict on Assisted Suicide Trial." *Washington Post*, November 23, 1996.

Walsh, Kerry-Anne. "Vote . . . Life, Death, Choice. Will to Die: Australians Expect the Freedom to Manage Their Lives—So Why Not Their Deaths?" *Bulletin*, September 17, 1996.

Ward, Russell. "Age and Acceptance of Euthanasia." Paper prepared for the Society for the Study of Social Problems, 1979.

Weijer, Charles. "Learning from the Dutch: Physician-Assisted Death, Slippery Slopes, and the Nazi Analogy." *Health-Law Review* 4 (1995): 23–29.

Wertham. *The German Euthanasia Program.* Cincinnati: Hayes Publishing, 1977.

Index

About the Authors

Jennifer M. Scherer, Ph.D., is vice president of research at the management consulting firm Association & Issues Management.

Rita J. Simon is a university professor in the School of Public Affairs and The Washington College at American University.